can i have (and do) it all, please?

. . . yes!

Published by Equip & Empower Ministries
Sydney, Australia.

First published 2009

Printed in China

National Library of Australia Cataloguing-in-Publication Entry

Author:	Caine, Christine.
Title:	Can I have and do it all, please? / Christine Caine.
Edition:	1st ed.
ISBN:	9780980518719 (pbk.)
Notes:	Bibliography.
Subjects:	Christian women--Conduct of life.
	Christian women--Life skills guides.
Dewey Number:	248.843

1 2 3 4 5 6 7 8 9 10 / 12 11 10 09

For more information about books and other teaching resources from Christine Caine, please contact Equip & Empower Ministries: PO Box 7820, Baulkham Hills BC, NSW 2153, Australia.

This book is dedicated to my husband and best friend, Nick, who I frequently refer to as the single most ravishing piece of masculine flesh on planet earth...and he never argues.

contents

prologue

prologue

I almost fell backwards off my stool from the explosion of voices directed straight at me. Luckily, I caught myself before I wound up on the floor of the platform, because me in a skirt, wrestling with the stool and trying to gracefully poise myself back into an upright position would not have been a pretty sight. *What has gotten into these women? I thought this would be a simple, straightforward Q&A session like I do at almost every other women's conference.* There was something different going on here. The women were on a mission to get some answers!

I tried to isolate a question from the cacophony of voices in the hope of trying to calm these women down with some insights, but it was impossible. They were speaking all at once. Finally, the MC was able to get everyone's attention and regain a semblance of order. Once settled, she realized that asking, "Who has a question for Christine?" was clearly not the way to go about this particular Q&A session. Instead she said, "If you have a question for Christine, please don't blurt it out; simply raise your hand and I will call on you."

Whoosh! A sea of hands immediately went up. I could feel the breeze on my face from the movement.

First Question: "Christine, how are you able to do everything that you do? Being a wife, a mother, a speaker, and everything else—can you give us some wisdom about how to balance our lives?"

Wow, I thought. *Couldn't we start with something easier like, "What's your favorite food?"* I took a deep breath and began to spill out some of the insights I felt God had given me throughout the years, which have become keys in my own life. It's a huge question, but I did my best to offer some personal thoughts and experiences.

With the question giver seemingly satisfied with my response, the MC asked for the next question. *Whoosh!* Again, hundreds of hands shot up, followed by the cool breeze on my cheeks.

Second Question: "Christine, I feel like I'm called to some kind of ministry. I'm a wife and a mom...how can I juggle all these roles and still accomplish everything God has for me to do?"

Isn't that kind of the same question as the first one? I thought. *Maybe I didn't answer it well enough first time round.* So this time I tried to give even more detail and wisdom about how I believe God wants us to live our lives *sane* whilst fulfilling all we have to do. This time I nailed it, or so I thought. There was a lot of nodding in agreement from the women in the room, as if to say they were really getting a lot out of what I was saying.

Time for the next question. *Whoosh!* Hundreds of hands. Cool breeze.

Third Question: "Christine, as I look at your life and ministry, I can see you have tapped into some knowledge about how to actually have and do all God has for you to have and do. Can you share with us how you are accomplishing it all?"

Have I entered the Twilight Zone? Isn't this the same question? Instead of answering this one, I thought I'd ask the ladies a question of my own. "Before I address that great question, I'd like to ask you all this: does anyone have a question that *does not* relate to 'how to have and do it all in life?'"

Silence. No *whoosh*. No hands. No breeze.

That's when it began to dawn on me. Women today are facing unprecedented challenges as our roles and influence continue to expand. Not all that long ago, the role of a woman was generally defined by the boundaries of her home, but today we have a much more active role to play in all aspects of society. Not only are we sister, daughter, wife and mother, but we are also teacher, salesperson, doctor, lawyer, politician, activist, business owner, writer, athlete, administrator and the list goes on and on and on. More than ever before, we women are navigating through increasing amounts of responsibility, activity, scheduling and multi-tasking...and we need some answers about how to have and do it all in life! The women with their questions that day were proof of this reality.

I soon discovered this was not an isolated incident. Over the next several months, on every continent, no matter where I traveled, this type of Q&A session became the norm. In a variety of languages and from girls in all seasons of life, I began to notice a common thread in their questions: these women wanted to know how they could have and do everything God has for them, and they wanted to know it now! As those months of answering the same questions turned into years, I thought, *Geez! Someone ought to write a book about this!* So here goes...

Admittedly, I don't have all the answers, nor do I have this thing called life perfectly figured out. Although, wouldn't that be nice?! However, I can say that after more than 40 years of life, 15 years of full-time ministry, over a decade of marriage and two children later—all the while juggling the unique challenges and opportunities of being a woman in today's world—I have learned some fundamental truths that have helped me navigate the journey of figuring out just how we *can* have and do all that God wants from us.

Can I Have And Do It All, Please? will give you a fresh perspective on womanhood and our precious value to God, as well as His unique plan for each of our lives. In this amazing journey of being a woman, the biggest lesson I've learned is when we are running after God, fully trusting in Him with our life, He gives us the grace and measure to have and to do it *all*... but maybe just not all at one time! Our God knows our particular seasons, and His timing is impeccable. Sometimes we just need to get used to synchronizing our watches to His. We absolutely can have and do it all in life, but first we have to discover some simple keys as to *how*.

So here is a peek into my life: some of my challenges, frustrations, hilarious moments and revelations of the timeless principles that have helped me realize it *is* possible to have and do it all!

it's all about all

chapter one
it's all about all

I woke up excited. Today was a new day, and yesterday's crazy attempt to accomplish my to-do list was long behind me. I knew things were looking up as I woke before my alarm went off, and I was actually able to take a shower before the girls got out of bed (which is more than I could say about the day before) I could just sense today was the day I would cross off all the tasks on my to-do list, and really, it had to be because there was so much I needed to do before I hit the road again. Granted, I couldn't remember the last time I was able to check every single item off my list—at least not since my girls were born—but being the eternal optimist, today was going to be "that" day!

I had every detail flawlessly mapped out. My workout clothes were already in the car so I could stop by the gym on the way home from driving Catie and Sophia to school and preschool (check). Catie's lunch was made and bagged, along with a special birthday gift for her teacher. Catie had told me how her teacher loved caramel apples, so I had bought some from the best place in town (check, check). We had a staff meeting scheduled over lunch to strategize the next few months for the ministry, and then my plan was to squeeze in a little writing just before picking up the girls, and driving home to cook dinner for the family. I had already gotten the groceries I needed to make supper (check), and while out, I had also happened to find a fun little nightgown to surprise my hubby at the end of the evening. That was going to be worth at least 15 checks!

Finally, my dream day was going to happen, and I was going to have it all. I had already succeeded in waking up on time and showering...nothing could stop me now! Today, I'd be Martha Stewart in the home, Arnold Schwarzenegger at the gym, Richard Branson at the office, Billy Graham in the ministry, Jane Austen at the computer, and lover extraordinaire in the bedroom. All that was left to do was to step out of my bedroom and begin my day.

And then Murphy's Law began...

First, the zipper on Catie's school pants broke and all her other pairs were in the laundry. *Do I have a sewing kit? Wait a minute, who am I kidding...do I even know how to work a needle and thread?* She would simply have to wear a skirt. Then, on the way to school, I was informed we were supposed to bring plates and napkins for the teacher's birthday party. We were already running late, thanks to the zipper incident, but I managed to speed across three lanes of traffic to an exit close to a grocery store, run in to buy the party necessities, and still get everyone to school in one piece.

The gym was packed, but I got in a pretty intense and sweaty workout before the electricity freakishly went out. Of course, this prevented me from washing and freshening up before my staff meeting. *Oh well, they've seen me without makeup before... no big deal.* On my way to the office, traffic was at a standstill because of the random power outage, which caused me to be extremely late to the lunch meeting, so I skipped eating. The schedule was now *way* behind, so I didn't have time to write, which was probably a good thing because after a hard work-out and no food, my brain was a bit fuzzy.

The rest of my afternoon was a whirlwind of activity: firstly navigated massive amounts of traffic to pick the girls up from their respective schools. Catie expressed her teacher's extreme surprise at my gift—*had the teacher forgotten she told me about her caramel apple fetish?* Next, helped the girls with their homework while simultaneously burning dinner. Tried to substitute the charred mess with leftovers—on closer inspection discovered they should have been thrown out days ago. Consequently, phoned Nick to pick up some take-out food. Lastly, I slipped into the bathtub whilst trying to give the girls their baths. *Thank God* Nick offered to put them to bed so I could have a moment of quiet before bedtime. I eagerly accepted and then collapsed into bed.

What in the world had gone wrong? I thought. *I had such high hopes that this day would be one where I would finally be able to do it all without having partial mental breakdown!!* I couldn't decide whether to laugh, cry, or throw something at the wall, and then I remembered...I still had that fun little nightgown to surprise Nick! Today didn't have to be a complete loss; maybe I could still be lover extraordinaire! I ran to the kitchen to grab the little bag holding my special purchase, whisked back to the bedroom, opened up the bag and pulled out...a pair of neatly wrapped caramel apples! No wonder Catie's teacher was so surprised!

It occurred to me in that one instant: perhaps my concept of "doing it all" was all wrong.

the utopian "all"

Okay, so this story is a little dramatic (only a bit), but most of us can in some way relate to this scenario. For years, we have been told we can have it all, be it all, and do it all. So inevitably, we have aggressively set out on a pursuit to achieve this utopian "all." We roll up our sleeves in true "Rosie the Riveter" style (to reveal our femininely chiseled arms, of course) and belt out the lyrics to "I Am Woman Hear Me Roar" in our best Helen Reddy voice. We get up an hour early to exercise, another hour earlier to pray, and a third hour is needed to get the kids ready and packed for school. We are consummate organizers, jugglers and problem solvers as we manage husbands, children, church commitments, friendships, finances, groceries, mealtimes, child taxi service, quiet time with God and whatever else is on the agenda. Then, at the end of the day we stay up an hour longer to ensure the house is tidy, an additional hour to read a chapter of the latest bestseller, and one more hour to ensure we spend "quality time" with our husband. It almost gets to the point that we should forego sleep altogether because the moment our head touches the pillow, it's time to rise and shine.

We've set out on this mission to do it "all" only to quickly discover that in order to achieve it, we conservatively need an extra 24 hours in every day. The fact is that the pursuit of having and doing it all has left many women disappointed, discouraged, exhausted, defeated, anxious and stressed. Despite our sometimes superhuman exploits, we begin to question the pace and fullness of this "having and doing it all" life and whether or not we have all been sold a big lie. In our disillusionment, we can even begin to think there is no possible way we can manage a strong Christian walk, an amazing marriage, great kids, a fulfilling sex life, fantastic friends and pursuing our God-given purpose.

The truth is, you *can* have it all, and you *can* do it all...but often it's an incorrect perception of what the "all" is that can leave us feeling like we fall short. If we want to do this adventure called life well, and fulfill the purpose God has for our lives, we need to discover what His definition of the "all" is, and go after that.

When I was a teenager, I really wanted to be a basketball player. Then reality hit: the statistical probability of a petite 5'2" girl making headlines because of her ability to slam-dunk a basketball was next to nothing. If I had chosen to ignore this fact and equated my "all" with being the next WNBA superstar, I would have wasted a lot of years with a relatively futile pursuit. The point is that each one of us has a specific "all" created especially for us, and if we pursue only this, God in turn enables us to achieve it.

Having it all does not mean we can have anything we want, or that we can have everything simultaneously. Nor should the media, politicians, the feminist movement, culture, history, the latest talk show host, lifestyle magazines, tradition, the latest celebrity, or our flesh dictate our pursuits, dreams and goals to us. It should be the result of seeking first the Kingdom of God.

In Matthew 6:33, Jesus says, *"But seek first the kingdom of God and his righteousness, and all these things will be added to you."*[1] When it's God who adds the "all" rather than us trying to strive for it on our own, we don't have to be stressed, overworked or anxious about trying to keep something we cannot obtain on our own anyway. If we simply continue to put God first, He adds it to our life according to His perfect will and His perfect timing.

Similarly, the Bible teaches that there are certain things God has created for each one of us to do. The book of Ephesians says, *"For we are God's [own] handiwork (His workmanship), recreated in Christ Jesus, [born anew] that we may do those good works which God pre-destined (planned beforehand) for us [taking paths which He prepared ahead of time], that we should walk in them [living the good life which He prearranged and made ready for us to live]."*[2]

If we spend our lives doing the good works God predestined for us, we will always find enough time, energy and resources to do it all. On the other hand, if we try to walk in paths God has not prepared for us, doing works He has not set out for us, we will inevitably end up living stressed, unfulfilled, frustrated and disappointed.

The "all" we should want to have and do is tied in to God Himself and His purpose for our lives. If we seek Him first always and align our lives with the good works He has prepared for us, it is truly amazing how our crazy, full-to-overflowing lives seem to work.

an interconnected, not compartmentalized life

Having established that the pursuit of the Kingdom of God, His righteousness and our God-ordained purpose is the foundation for having and doing it all, we now need to figure out how this really works in our everyday lives.

I have found most things in life come back to Emeril Lagasse's Chocolate Cocoa-Buttermilk Cake with Chocolate Icing. Let me explain. I want you to think of this chocolate cake recipe that Emeril whipped up to celebrate Good Morning America's five-year anniversary in New York City's Time Square studio.

In order to make this cake you will need:
- 14 tablespoons unsalted butter, softened
- 2 cups plus 2 tablespoons all-purpose flour
- ¾ cup unsweetened cocoa powder
- 1¼ teaspoons baking soda
- ½ teaspoon salt
- 1¼ cups buttermilk

- 2 tablespoons brewed espresso or strong coffee, cooled
- 1 teaspoon pure vanilla extract
- 1¾ cups packed light brown sugar
- 2 large eggs
- chocolate icing

You simply could not make this cake without every ingredient listed above, yet when a piece of cake is sitting before you with an oversized dollop of whipped cream on the side, the last thing on your mind is the list of individual ingredients that went into making the cake. You're only thinking of the combined result you're just about to sit back and devour.

However, the truth is that the cake is made up of many different ingredients, all of which are key to its success. Every cake starts with a measure of flour and then various other ingredients depending upon what kind of cake it's going to become. If you removed any one of its parts, the overall result would be affected in terms of flavor and consistency. Once baked, it's impossible to isolate the flour from the eggs, or the milk from the chocolate. It's all mixed together, and that's what makes the cake so wonderful.

Similarly, every area of our life is interconnected and mixed together: spiritual, relational, emotional and physical. The whole, which is who we are, is the net sum total of each of these parts. Just like each cake starts out with a measure of flour as its foundation, our "all" begins with Jesus at the center of our lives. Then, depending upon what kind of "cake" we are to be, all of the other components are added accordingly.

Simultaneously, I am a Christian, a mother, a wife, a daughter, a sister, a friend, a pastor, a preacher, an author and all of the other facets that make me the kind of "cake" that I am. Every "ingredient" of my life is interconnected. I don't stop being a mother when I'm preaching, nor do I stop being a wife when I am bathing the children, just as I don't stop being a Christian when I'm having a "discussion" with my husband. I'm all of these all of the time, and they all work together to make me who I am. My life begins to spiral out of control when I try to separate, isolate and compartmentalize these areas, rather than keeping them interconnected. I need to allow all of the components that make me who I am to work synergistically to create the God-life I'm called to live.

I used to wrongly think that as a good Christian woman, my priorities in life had to be in the following order:

1. God
2. Family
3. Church
4. Career/Work
5. Ministry/Service
6. Friends
7. Leisure
8. Health/Fitness

It's not that there's anything wrong with these priorities or the order I chose to put them in, but instead of seeing my life as an interconnected whole, I had set things up in competition with each other. I was constantly frustrated because I never seemed to have enough time for anything, especially God, and He was at the top of my list! I could not devote enough time to all (or sometimes any) of the items on my list; therefore I was *never* able to check off one "task" and confidently move on to the next (especially in the "right" order).

The reason things did not fit into my neatly constructed box or list of priorities was because, well, life happens! The kids don't always want to eat their veggies in five minutes or go to bed at 8pm sharp or even get straight As at school. Your computer crashes and you lose your entire day's work. Your husband has had a tough day and would prefer to watch the game rather than spend quality time with you. Someone becomes ill or a tragedy strikes. The reality is that unexpected events and disruptions occur daily, and no matter how much we try to control things, we ultimately can't control every moment of every day.

When you compartmentalize your life like I did mine, you set yourself up for feeling like a clown juggling a thousand balls at once, all the while waiting for the whole act to come raining down all around you. We can convince ourselves that if we focus on being a better wife, our kids will be neglected in the process. Or if we pursue our career, there will be less time for church and friends. Or if we spend time with our family, then we are not spending time with God. So every time we try to develop one area, we secretly feel guilty for neglecting another. Our life becomes one big mess of competing priorities.

God never intended for life to be a juggling act, nor for us to feel that if we nurture one aspect of our lives, it will be at the expense of another. The different aspects of our lives are not supposed to compete against each other because each is valid and necessary, and together, make us who we are.

super woman or super natural?

I always dreamed of being Wonder Woman. I tried jumping off my garage roof a few times, complete with a cape and my underwear on the outside of my pants only to get to the roof and realize I've always been scared of heights. I thought Wonder Woman could do anything; and those gold wrist-bands—if only I had a pair of them—I could have achieved the impossible!

My aspirations of becoming a superhero came to naught, as countless other little girls' dreams have, but aren't there days in our lives when we feel like we have to be a super woman if we're going to get through it alive? Sometimes it can seem like everybody wants a piece of you: your kids want lunch and want to be driven to sports training, your boss needs that report, your mom says you never visit, your friend is on the phone because her marriage is in crisis, you have bills to pay, dinner to cook, and when you finally think the day is over and you climb under the covers, your husband wants to make love!

The "secret" I'm about to reveal won't eliminate these kinds of days (disappointing, I know), but it will take the stress out of living through them. The secret (drum roll, please) is: you don't have to be a super woman, you just need to be supernatural!

In Proverbs 31, we see a picture of a supernatural woman. This woman was an excellent wife and mother, she worked diligently, provided food for her family, rose early, was an entrepreneur, she dressed immaculately, helped the poor and the needy, and was wise, kind, strong and dignified. The fact that this woman exists in the Bible, and long before cell phones, computers and dishwashers, shows us that we can have and do it all in life without having a nervous breakdown.

I understand that for some of us, simply reading about this Proverbs 31 woman can make us feel tired, weary and stretched to capacity. Rather than motivating us, she only serves to remind us of how much we are *not* doing. However, I see this woman not as a superhero but rather as one who sets the standard for every Christian woman. In the midst of a normal life, she discovered a secret—the God factor—and came to realize she didn't need to be superhuman at all, but supernaturally empowered by the Holy Spirit. Through His strength, wisdom and endurance, she was able to have and do her "all." As a result, within the context of her family and her world, she enlarged her capacity to live the abundant life God wanted her to live.

And this abundant "Proverbs 31" life is exactly what God deeply desires for every one of His girls. He wants us to learn how to tap into the supernatural empowerment of the Holy Spirit because this is the only way we will be able to fulfill our God-purpose and destiny without burning out or giving up along the way. The Holy Spirit is the helper Jesus promised would be with us always,[3] and He will enable us to live the supernatural life. With Him and through Him, we really can be like the Proverbs 31 woman and be able to have and do it all, despite the screaming children, traffic jams, work deadlines, sleep deprivation, laundry piles, date nights...and the list continues.

God's "all" for your life is right before you, ready to be seized, enjoyed, bring you tremendous fulfillment, and stretch you to your limits! You absolutely *can* have and do it all, and live the life you've dreamed of...if you understand that your "all" will be a journey of a lifetime, and that sometimes your "all" can shift and morph when you least expect it.

The next three chapters will focus on how you can build the strong foundation needed to experience the "having and doing it all" kind of life, whilst the final few chapters share some wisdom about how to balance and build the endurance needed for this exciting adventure of destiny.

No matter where you're at in life right now, where you've come from, or what you may have experienced, God has an "all" designed specifically for you to embrace so you can become a force that can change your world!

it's all about value

chapter two
it's all about value

I was on a warpath. My objective: to purge my household. My weapons: trash bags, boxes and my keen awareness for unnecessary clutter. My victims: quite simply any item that had not been used, worn or played with in the previous 48 hours... Okay, we'll make it an even 72 hours. Sounds a bit obsessive? Perhaps. But I'm a purger, and to be perfectly honest, for me purging is absolutely cathartic!

I'm quite well known for these tendencies; in fact, my team has even coined the phrase "the three degrees of the CCP (Chris Caine Purge)." Let me break it down for you. The first degree of the CCP is known as the "unidentifiable object purge." The only way I can explain this phenomenon is that God must have divinely implanted in me a homing device that, even after several weeks of traveling the world, gives me the ability to step inside my house and immediately detect an object that wasn't there before I left. It can be the tiniest object, and even completely out of eyesight. It's as if I walk in, take a look around, and within seconds, the hair on the back of my neck gets prickly and an almost audible alarm goes off inside my head. "Alert! Unidentifiable object is present. Must...purge... *now*!!"

In compulsive obedience to this inner voice, I will casually inch my way toward the unwanted object, all the while continuing to share my newest plan for evangelizing the planet before the second coming of Christ with everyone present. You see, this homing device is innate, almost a sixth sense, and comes as easily as breathing. Once I have located the object and put it in its proper place (usually the trash can), equilibrium and order are restored, and the urge to purge is satisfied.

The second degree of the CCP is called the "in-out purge," and is the most popular among all those around me. Anytime I obtain something new, whether it be a gift or an item I purchased myself, something else has to go. I can't tell you how many times people from my team have left my house carrying furniture, tableware, clothes and many other random items. If something is coming in, then something else *must* go out!

Finally, there is the infamous "mass purge." During one of these spells, essentially any item on the Caine property not possessing a pulse is in danger of being thrown out or given away. In my mind, cleanliness is somewhere right up there with godliness, and the "mass purge" is essential for this kind of living. Not to mention, the amazing joy this aspect of the CCP brings to me.

By noon that day, I was in full "mass purge" mode. I had nearly been through every room in the house, and had amassed a large stockpile of purged items I couldn't wait to rid my life of. These included: kids' clothes, furniture, utensils, toys and pets. (Oh! For all you animal lovers, I meant only Chia pets... I'm not usually home long enough to keep *either* kind alive!) There was only one small zone that remained untouched, and this holy ground was Nick's closet. I will admit that the thought did cross my mind that I should wait until he was home to purge his area, but I quickly brushed it off, thinking that after a long day at work, he certainly wasn't going to want to take the time to clean. Besides, Nick is a bit purge-challenged. So, in the spirit of cleanliness, I dove in. Anything I thought was no longer of value to us was tossed into a pile. In a matter of moments, and a flurry of shirts, socks and shoes, I had a large pile of rejects.

In the midst of all this activity, I came across an old fob watch. *Where in the world did this come from?* I wondered, as I noticed it had been made before I was even born and looked like it hadn't worked in decades. (It didn't occur to me maybe it simply needed to be wound.) I decided it had no value—*certainly that two-inch diameter of space could be used for something far more effective*—and I just threw the watch right on top of the large, glorious purge pile. With that, the job was done.

That night, Nick came home, and as he went to kiss the girls goodnight, he saw the boxes containing purged toys and clothes. Knowingly he laughed, all too aware of what kind of tornado had swept through the house that day. We were attending a special dinner that night, and since there were only a few minutes before we had to leave, Nick went into the closet to grab a clean shirt. After a few minutes of rustling, he made his way downstairs toward the pile that came from his closet. There must be a shirt he wanted to un-purge! The purge security alarms started sounding off inside my head, and I just had to go down and help him understand the fundamental rules of the "mass purge." I was about to give him the "why are you trying to hoard trash" speech when I saw everything about his demeanor change. The shirt Nick was holding dropped to the floor as he slowly went to pick something else up from the pile. It was the fob watch. He turned around and noticed me standing there, and as tears began to stream down his face, he began to tell me the story of the watch. Nick was very close to his father, who tragically died on Nick's 19th birthday. This watch was one of the only things Nick had left from his father. It was of great value to Nick—a precious memento of their relationship. Because of me, it could have been lost forever.

what is value?

I will never forget the look on Nick's face as he picked up the watch, or how terrible I felt for not realizing what it meant to him. In my flurry of activity that day, I had considered it worthless and wanted to throw it away. I learned a great lesson from that experience: if we don't understand the value of something we will often mistreat, abuse and discard that thing.

As sad as it would have been if I had thrown away an item that held sentimental value for Nick, sadder still is the fact that every day, countless humans are mistreated and discarded for simply being women. This is a reality we see in the work we do with young women in Eastern Europe that have been the victims of human trafficking. Many of these young girls believe they are pursuing employment in Western Europe, with the hope they will make something more of their lives. Often living in poverty in remote villages, they think their best chance for any kind of future is to find work outside their country. They are lured by traffickers, and often tricked into believing they will be employed legitimately, but instead they are trafficked, beaten and forced to become sex slaves. Traffickers see them only in terms of their perceived economic value, not as human beings who have hopes, dreams and aspirations. They are often tortured and imprisoned, forced to perform degrading acts, beaten and humiliated.

Throughout history, and in almost every culture and tradition, we see examples of where women have been devalued. Plato, the classical Greek Philosopher wrote, *"We cannot escape the pain for it lives among us. It is our sisters, mothers, our betrothed, our wives, our daughters, our mistresses, our concubines. Furthermore, if we spend our lives in wrongdoing and cowardice, afterward Zeus will send us back into life as a woman."* Similarly, his student, Aristotle, who he clearly taught "well" wrote, *"The female is a monstrosity, a deformed male, and deformity which occurs in the ordinary core of nature."* Finally, although there are countless other examples, an old Jewish prayer, the "beraka," states, *"Blessed be he who did not make me a gentile. Blessed be he who did not make me a woman. Blessed be he who did not make me an uneducated man or slave."*[1]

Unfortunately these perceptions of women are not reserved to the history books. Despite the enormous strides women have made over the last 200 years in many nations, there are still many cultures today where women are considered as the inferior sex. They are deemed as second-class citizens, objects simply for sensual gratification, weak and emotional beings lacking in intelligence and therefore have nothing to contribute to society. They are seen by many as the personal property of men, the equivalent of cattle, personal servants, domestic slaves and subhuman beings.

Some shocking statistics include:

- Each day, 6,000 women are genitally mutilated in North Africa.
- More than 15,000 women will be sold into sexual slavery in China this year.
- 200 women in Bangladesh will be horribly disfigured when their spurned husbands or suitors burn them with acid.
- More than 7,000 women in India will be murdered by their families and in-laws in disputes over dowries.
- At least one out of every three women in the world is likely to be beaten, coerced into sex or otherwise abused in her lifetime.
- One in five women will become a victim of rape or attempted rape.[2]

Is it any wonder that some of us have had a difficult time feeling valuable as women? I mention these examples not as some battle cry for us all to whip off our bras and reach for a match, but simply to point out that engrafted in the fabric of almost all of our cultures is a belief that the women are less than, weaker to, and of lesser value to men. Knowing this can help us to understand why some of us can at times struggle with feeling inferior.

God values us equally

It's incomprehensible that women continue to be perceived and treated this way. It's a far cry from God's original purpose for womanhood. When God created woman, He did not create her as an afterthought, or as second best.

The Bible teaches us, *"God created man in his own image, in the image of God he created him; male and female he created them."*[3] This original spirit man that God created possessed all of the qualities of the masculine and the feminine. In Genesis 2, God took this spirit man and placed it into two physical forms: the male and the female, for the purpose of fulfilling His eternal plan on the earth. In fact, God created Eve out of the same substance from which He created Adam; that's why the Bible says, *"She was taken out of man."*[4] Eve was not a separate creation, but a separate expression of the same creation. From the outset, it is clear that God didn't make either the male or the female superior: they were both created from the same spirit-man and are of the same essence.

Essentially, man and woman are equal, but definitely different. We know this because God said, *"It is not good that man should be alone; I will make him a helper comparable to him."*[5] Note that God didn't say, "I'll make a slave for him" or a "mistress" or a "baby incubator." He called Eve a "helper." In the Hebrew, this word is *e'zer* which refers to someone who is strong, with no connotations to weakness. In fact, *e'zer* is often a word used to describe a characteristic of God. When He created the woman, it was not as a subordinate *for* man, but as a completer *to* man; someone who, united with Adam, would be equally responsible for fulfilling God's purpose.

When I first became a Christian, I had no concept of my value as a woman. I had been abused, and because of my feelings of rejection and pain, I had spent many years trying to desperately earn my sense of value. I thought that if I worked hard enough and achieved enough, I would somehow feel more valued by those around me. I wasted many years of my life doing a lot of activities that led to nothing but years of frustration and emptiness.

As I began to study the Scriptures, I found that during Jesus' ministry, He had encountered many women not unlike myself. He did not reject them, but lifted them up regardless of their past, forgave them, healed them, and encouraged them on a journey of becoming whole. He gave a place for women to prosper and to take an active part in His ministry. He always treated them with honor, dignity and grace, as if they were equal in value to men. I saw that Jesus had an unconditional and indescribable love for all people, both men and women, and it was this revelation that captured my heart and began my own healing process.

Jesus consistently placed value on women and womanhood, even though He lived and ministered in a culture where women were seen as inferior to men. Unmarried women were not allowed to leave their home without their father, and married women were not allowed to leave without their husband. (I would not have made it three days past my wedding day without getting stoned to death!) In addition, their heads were to be doubly veiled anytime they entered a public venue, and they were not allowed to speak to male strangers. Despite the social norms, Jesus boldly included women as a part of His life and ministry.

In addition, there is no recorded account in which Jesus avoided women, rebuked them for listening to His teaching, or healed all the men first before He decided if there was enough time to throw a few miracles in the general direction of the women. His arms were open to all; His healing was given to all to receive; His ministry was available for all to hear. In fact, we see Jesus giving women a place of leadership in his ministry: *"Now it came to pass, afterward, that He went through every city and village, preaching and bringing the glad tidings of the kingdom of God. And the twelve were with Him, and certain women who had been healed of evil spirits and infirmities—Mary called Magdalene, out of whom had come seven demons, and Joanna the wife of Chuza, Herod's steward, and Susanna, and many others who provided for Him from their substance."*[6] These women traveled alongside the 12 male disciples, and they were even instrumental in funding Jesus' ministry which I'm sure messed with the minds of a few of the religious leaders of the day!

In John 4, we read about how Jesus engaged in a conversation with a Samaritan woman. This was a faux pas of double proportions, firstly because she was a woman, and secondly, because she was an "unclean" Samaritan—oh, how the Jews *hated* the Samaritans! Yet Jesus ignored these social and cultural barriers. Not only did He ask her to give Him some water, He also proceeded to reveal her life story to her and how she could turn away from her current sin. He cared for her, saw her as valuable, and wanted to help heal her soul. Then, to top it all off, Jesus reveals to her that He is the Christ! This is the very first recorded account of Jesus telling anyone that He is the Messiah, and it is to an outcast Samaritan *woman*!

Again, in John 8, we read how Jesus intervened to rescue a woman about to be stoned to death after being caught in the act of adultery. In Luke 7, Jesus raises from the dead the only son of a widow, giving her a hope and a future. Unsurprisingly, these women became the very first preachers of the Gospel!

Jesus' behavior toward women was revolutionary, and I can only imagine, appalling and scandalous to most people. So why did He do it? Surely it would have been easier and more acceptable to stick to the conventions of the day. The truth is that Jesus came to reconcile *all* of humanity back to the Father, not just the men. The book of Galatians says, *"For as many [of you] as were baptized into Christ [into a spiritual union and communion with Christ, the Anointed One, the Messiah] have put on (clothed yourselves with) Christ. There is [now no distinction] neither Jew nor Greek, there is neither slave nor free, there is not male and female;* **for you are all one in Christ Jesus.***"*[7]

To Jesus, gender was (and is) a non-issue. He gifts, anoints and empowers us all without regard to race, creed or gender. All of humanity, male and female, is of equal value to God. We see this expressed in the fact that God gave His only begotten Son, Jesus Christ, as a ransom for us all. There could be no greater expression of His love for us, or how valuable we are to Him.

true value is never lost

In the early 1990s, there was a huge stir in art communities all over the world when a famous Caravaggio painting, considered to be lost for 200 years, was rediscovered on the wall of a Jesuit's home in Dublin, Ireland. The painting, *The Taking of Christ*, was a masterpiece by one of Italy's most famous and influential Baroque painters, and it disappeared in the late 18th century. Through a series of exciting events, starting with a random discovery by two graduate students in Rome and ending with an elder art scholar visiting a Jesuit priest's Dublin home, the painting was recovered.

For many years, it had been wrongly identified as a painted replica by another artist, and as a result, had been devalued and passed casually through several hands before landing on the Jesuit's wall. When it was found, there still was a question of its authenticity, but as layers of dirt and discolored varnish were painstakingly removed, the high technical quality of the painting was revealed. This became proof that the painting was actually the masterpiece crafted by Caravaggio over 300 years earlier, and this work of art, once considered only nominally valuable, became an extremely precious and priceless treasure. This painting will never again be thought of as cheap or second-rate.

To God, *you* are His masterpiece, and *you* are extremely precious to Him. Yes, today you might feel like you are used goods; maybe you have been hurt and damaged by your own poor choices or abused and discarded by people who did not understand your true value. But none of these circumstances have ever changed God's perception of your priceless value. While Caravaggio's painting hung for decades on that old, dank wall, many people saw it and were ignorant of its true value but this did not change the fact that it actually was an irreplaceable artistic masterpiece. The painting simply needed someone with a trained eye to recognize it and take the time to restore it to its original condition.

No matter how covered you think you are with layers of the world's dirt, grime and pain, God has always had a plan to restore you to your original and priceless value. His eye has been focused on you since the day you were conceived in your mother's womb, and His desire has always been to bring you back to the image in which He originally created you...which is His own image. It is only when you understand your true value that you can begin to have and do all that God has for you...because sometimes all it takes is realizing that you're worth it.

it's all about purpose

chapter three
it's all about purpose

You would have thought we were standing in front of the Ark of the Covenant or something. Everyone around me was talking in such hushed and reverent tones; I was convinced this moment was becoming a religious experience for them all. Granted, the thing *was* incredibly shiny; I could not figure out how they were able to keep it so immaculately clean. Plus, I'm sure if the sun hit it just right, the blinding glare could be mistaken as the presence of God. But try as I may, no matter how I looked at it, I just could not see it for anything other than what it really was: a super-duper, oversized, deep fat fryer.

I was 18 and standing with my future in-laws as they were explaining to me how their son would soon be taking over the family business: a restaurant with the best fish and chips in town. They were so proud of the inheritance they were going to leave him, and thought I would be ecstatic about the promising future we had in store. It was the eve of my high school final exams, and the purpose of this meeting was to lure me away from my "crazy" dreams of going on to university. I was told in no uncertain terms that the only way the marriage ceremony would occur was if I abandoned my plans for further education, as back in those days, a Greek wife couldn't be more educated than her husband; it just wasn't done (at least in this family). What's more, why would I need further education to fulfill what they thought was my purpose in life, or procreation and good housekeeping? Besides, how could a future filled with college and a career *possibly* compare to becoming Con's wife?

As everyone was talking a mile a minute, so excited about the glorious deep fat fryer, I had one of those out-of-body experiences. Everybody's voice faded away and all I could hear was the dialogue going on inside my head. In my 18-year-old mind, there was just so much to consider, and the thought of having to make a choice between a marriage and family (both of which I really wanted) and a college degree (which I also *really* wanted) seemed overwhelming.

On one hand, every single one of the female role models in my family had foregone university and married very young, and they all seemed content raising their children and tending to household chores. Certainly, all those women proved that I could have a very fulfilled life if I married Con, right? I desired having a family; if I turned down this proposal, would it jeopardize my chances later?

On the other hand, I never did quite feel I fit into that mold. Even at a very young age, I preferred books to Barbies, playing soccer with the boys to ballet classes, and sneakers to high heels. My mother was always saying to me, "Christina, why can't you be like all the other girls? Why can't you be normal and want what everyone else wants?"

Another thing that played on my mind was the impact that refusing the proposal would have on my family. Would I bring disgrace and shame to them? Would we be able to mend our relationship if I turned my back on my family's tradition and culture? Would going after my dreams be worth it if it meant falling out with my family whom I loved dearly? Don't get me wrong; it wasn't that my family was actively trying to limit or thwart my purpose or potential, it's simply that I was the daughter of Greek migrants, and Greek culture and tradition dictated very strict stereotypes and protocols for what was appropriate for a woman. Of course this experience is in no way every Greek girl's experience, but it was mine.

Despite the firm gender stereotyping of my culture and tradition, I could not shake this undeniable sense that I was on the earth for a purpose unique to me. As I was lost in thought, standing in the fish and chip store that day, I knew that it was a defining moment for me. Whatever I chose would alter my life forever, and there would be no turning back.

When I shared the above story with some of the young women in my office, they laughed that I actually had to choose between university and marriage at 18 years old! In fact, one of the American girls on my team, Natalie, grew up with an entirely different experience from mine. Her mother is a college graduate and a successful business owner, who in Natalie's own words, "has never picked up a broom, cleaned a bathroom, or done a load of laundry in her life." When Natalie went on to university after high school, this was the norm; in fact, it was expected. Had she desired to marry and become a stay-at-home mom at 18, it would have been frowned upon and vehemently discouraged, as there were many glass ceilings yet to be shattered.

From both my experience and Natalie's, it is evident that many of our preconceptions of the purpose and potential of a woman have been established by our upbringing, tradition, culture, role models and our parents' expectation. The simple truth is, if we are to have and do it all in life, we cannot be limited by all of these things, rather we need to seek out God's purpose for our lives.

The Bible clearly teaches us God has put a divinely implanted sense of purpose on the inside of each and every one of us. Ecclesiastes 3:11 tells us, *"He has made everything beautiful in its time. He also has planted eternity in men's hearts and minds [a **divinely implanted sense of a purpose** working through the ages which nothing under the sun but God alone can satisfy], yet so that men cannot find out what God has done from the beginning to the end."*[1]

I can safely assume that if you are reading this book, you have a desire to have and do it all in life. Therefore, let me share with you one of the most fundamental and profound keys that will enable you to do this: we must ensure our "all" is actually the purpose God had in mind when He created us. If you try to pursue any other "all," you will never be satisfied. I believe I ultimately turned down Con's marriage proposal because I had an inner sense that there had to be more. I did not know what this "more" was, nor did I have any idea I would be doing what I am doing today. I simply had to let go of any model or stereotype I had known up until that point, step out in faith, and embrace the greater purpose for which God had put me on the earth. In the same way, you must ensure you do not settle for anything less than God's ultimate purpose and plan for your life.

your unique "life-print"

It is no coincidence God gave each of us a distinct set of markings unique to every person alive or who has ever lived: the fingerprint. Even identical twins aren't 100% identical because each has a different pattern on their fingertips. I believe this is one of the ways God reminds us that each of us is an original, a unique person with a unique purpose. Psalm 139 says:

> "Oh yes, you shaped me first inside, then out; you formed me in my mother's womb. I thank you, High God—you're breathtaking! Body and soul, I am marvelously made! I worship in adoration—what a creation! You know me inside and out, you know every bone in my body; You know exactly how I was made, bit by bit, how I was sculpted from nothing into something. Like an open book, you watched me grow from conception to birth; all the stages of my life were spread out before you. The days of my life all prepared before I'd even lived one day."[2]

I love that! Just as God gave us fingerprints, He prepared for each of us a "life-print" that is completely our own.

Sadly, many women never truly discover there's a divine "life-print" for their life because they're too busy trying to "fit" into someone else's. This is as silly as Cinderella's stepsisters' attempts to stuff their big feet into the glass slipper. Remember that story? They so desperately wanted to fulfill a purpose that never was meant for them in the first place, and they both went to extreme measures to squeeze their fat feet into that slipper. In fact, in the original version of the story, they even cut off a few toes to try to make them fit! And before you get too grossed out, haven't we all gone to some pretty harsh measures to make that pair of designer shoes that were 75 per cent off—and three sizes too small—fit?

a big batch of comparison

The challenge that most of us face is the tendency to devalue our own uniqueness, and instead attempt to become a carbon copy of those we admire. We look at others who we deem to be "successful" or godly, Christian women, and rather than taking principles from their lives and applying them to our own, we try to become exactly like them. Ultimately, this leads to frustration because those shoes just weren't made for us!

I remember how on one occasion after a particularly grueling time on the road, I was tired and began looking around at how other women were living their Christian lives. I wanted the normality of sleeping in my own bed for more than a few days a month, of not getting on an airplane every other day, and of establishing something resembling a routine.

I wasn't exactly sure what a "normal life" would look or feel like, but I had convinced myself that it would be much easier than my current life. (Isn't it amazing how we always think the grass is greener on the other side of the fence?) Besides, surely God didn't want me to be feeling so stretched and so uncomfortable, did He? I mean, having and doing it all shouldn't leave me feeling this tired...it should be easy and fun and no big deal, right? I decided it was time for Christine Caine the preacher, teacher, wife, mother, crazy traveler etc. to change *everything*. I didn't want to have and do "my" all anymore, so I thought I would try someone else's.

So, the new Christine decided to start with baking! After dropping Catie off at school, and being inspired by seeing one of the mothers bringing in a plate of home-made cookies for a birthday party, I determined that from then on I was going to be the kind of mom that bakes cookies for her daughter to take to school. I remember thinking to myself, *imagine if I did not travel so much, I could be the best cookie maker on earth – I mean with all my Greek heritage flowing through my veins, wasn't it part of my DNA to be the pastry cook extraordinaire?*

Not to try and scale the mountain all at once, I bought a box of Mrs. Field's cookie mix; all I had to do was add one egg, some oil and water, and stir. Easy enough, right? All that was left to do was follow the simple directions:

1. Preheat oven. I'd never worked the oven before, so this presented a minor problem. However, after about 2 minutes of pressing buttons, I accidentally turned it on. Done.

can i have and do it all, please?

2. Add egg, oil, water and stir. What is the difference between a tablespoon and a cup? I wasn't sure. I just went ahead and used a cup for both. Also, what kind of oil do I use? I had about 4 different kinds in the cupboard. Being Greek, I quickly realized that a strong olive oil would be the best. Done.

3. Drop onto cookie sheet and place into the oven. Easy. Done.

4. Bake 12 minutes. No problem, I'll set the timer. Done.

Now all I had to do was wait for the timer to go off. I felt very proud of myself as I sat down on the couch. My girls were napping, I was baking; this was going to be a typical day in my new life. Just then, my BlackBerry went off and I began to respond to my email. Looking back, I do recall smelling something distinctly like smoke, but I just kept typing. Suddenly, the smoke alarms were blaring, my kitchen looked and smelled like a coal-burning locomotive had been driven through it, and my frightened girls were running down the stairs. I rushed them out onto the front lawn and watched as smoke billowed out of my kitchen windows. As I stood there with tears streaming down my cheeks, feeling like a complete failure, I realized that any chance of me volunteering in the school cafeteria was now up in smoke!

Later that night after putting the girls to bed, I distinctly heard the Lord ask me, "Who exactly are you trying to be?" I sat down to spend some time with God so He could help me make some sense out of the last few days. He simply reminded me that He had made Christine Caine unique from every other person on this planet and that being unique is okay; in fact, it's His intention. I felt God say to me, "The reason you are not like someone else is because I don't need another 'someone else'—I need a unique you." Instantly, I felt like a weight had been lifted off my shoulders, and I realized that just because I'm not super-cookie-baker-extraordinaire, it doesn't mean I'm not exactly the kind of woman God created me to be. The reason I had become discontent in my life was because I had allowed my focus to shift off pursuing my own unique life-print and onto the life-prints of some of the women around me.

This experience taught me that nothing good comes from comparing our unique call from God with someone else's. 2 Corinthians says, *"For we dare not class ourselves or compare ourselves with those who commend themselves. But they, measuring themselves by themselves, and comparing themselves among themselves, are not wise."*[3] Ladies, we definitely want to be wise women, so let's decide we are going to discover God's life-print for our life and fulfill it. We are each graced for our particular race and not anyone else's.

how to discover your unique "all"?

Okay, so let me be brutally honest with you for a second. If you haven't figured out already after reading about my cookie baking endeavors, I'm not exactly what you would call a domestic goddess...or at least not what the world defines one as. To add to the list of things that are not necessarily my unique "all" are: a worship-leader (I'm completely tone deaf), WWF wrestler (I'm pretty sure I would just die) and a career in the WNBA (I'm barely 5'2"). The funny thing is, I think for a split second at some point in life, I've wanted to pursue each one of these even though they are totally contrary to the way I am wired.

There is very little more frustrating than trying to force yourself into doing and becoming something you were never created for. The truth is that finding your unique purpose is not really as complex as you may think. You'll find your purpose is normally aligned with your gifts, talents and heart's desires. God designed and equipped us for the purpose of working through us to touch a lost and a broken world. Basically our talents, passions, gifts and interests are like a road map to discovering our unique life-print.

For me, I can distinctly remember a season when I was desperately trying to work out what my particular purpose in life was. I would talk and talk and talk and talk and talk about it... and then talk some more. It wasn't until one of my mentors said, "Uh, Christine, as immense a word quota you seem to have, don't you think you're probably called to be a communicator?" I remember thinking, *What? Doesn't everyone talk this fast and furious? Isn't everyone as passionate to talk about the Word for hours upon hours?* It began to become clear to me that the very things I was both passionate about and naturally gifted for were directly tied into the unique life-print with which God had created me.

Did I step into the specifics immediately? Absolutely not! It was definitely a process (and still is). With each season of obedience, different aspects of my unique life-print become more defined. I think this is one of the most exciting qualities of our individual call; it's an unfolding adventure.

If you have been struggling with uncertainty about what unique gifts you bring to the table of life, here are 15 questions to ask yourself. These will help you sift through all the desires in your heart and separate the God-given dreams from the "that would be kinda cool" fantasies. Ask yourself:

1. What is it that I've been good at since an early age?
2. What do others look at me doing that would be hard for them, but seems effortless to me?
3. What is it that I consistently find myself sharing about or helping others with?
4. Why do I think God created me?
5. What am I most passionate about?
6. What things enrage me and what problems in the world do I have a passion, over and above all others, to solve?
7. What subjects could I talk about for hours and days without a loss of momentum?
8. What Scriptural truths and subjects have been those that most bear witness to me and speak life to me?
9. What have been the biggest struggles I have encountered in life?
10. What have been my biggest victories and breakthroughs? Why?
11. What subjects or topics do I enjoy learning about?
12. What would I be doing if money wasn't an issue?

13. What type of people do I connect with easily or have compassion for?

14. What were my favorite subjects in high school or college?

15. What part of the globe or cultures do I have a passion for?

I believe that as you meditate upon your answers—even discuss them with strong and mature Christians around you—you will find greater clarity. After you answer these, ask yourself what are the next steps you need to take in order to nurture and develop these passions and interests you have. Commit to a lifetime of learning and growing.

Once we discover our unique "all," our lives become even richer and more exciting as we quickly learn that having and doing it all is not just about us, it's about helping and serving others. We begin to clearly see how our specific destiny is a God-ordained puzzle piece that fits perfectly into His strategy for reaching the lost and the hurting during this moment in time. We have the awesome responsibility of recognizing and developing the gifts on our lives because they were given to us by God in order to impact the world around us. We need to ask ourselves: *If I do not step up and run my race, who may not end up hearing about Jesus? Who may remain hungry? Who may remain enslaved, impoverished or forsaken...or who may miss out on simply discovering that they too have a unique "all?"*

Let's determine in our hearts to seek to discover our unique purpose. There's nothing more exciting than living each day having and doing all that we were perfectly designed to do, *and* there's no use wasting even a second of our time trying to jam our foot into someone else's glass slipper...we have a world to change!!

it's all about identity

chapter four
it's all about identity

One of my friends has spent over a decade of her life pursuing a career on stage as a singer, dancer and actress. We were talking recently and she had me laughing hysterically as she recounted some of the craziest—and most embarrassing—stories that happened on stage during some of her performances.

While playing the tough girl character, *Rizzo*, from the musical *Grease*, she accidentally set her fake fingernails on fire while trying to light a cigarette (clearly, she'd never smoked a day in her life). In a different performance of the same show, her wig got snagged on a piece of scenery as she was dancing in the finale, and the hairpiece bubbled up several inches on top of her head. Even though she looked like Marge Simpson, and the audience couldn't contain their laughter, she had to keep dancing and singing until the curtain went down. On another occasion, whilst she was performing in a children's musical, a couple dozen of the boys in the audience got so involved with the suspense of the play that they actually stormed the stage to beat up the bad guy and save the day for her character!

However, the best story was about the musical in which she had 24 costume changes in the course of a two-hour show. She was playing several different comedic characters, each one having a very specific and identifiable costume. With each stage entrance, the audience would recognize the character based upon what she was wearing, and with each exit, all mayhem would break loose backstage as she had to frantically change from head to toe in order to make it back onstage in as little as 60 seconds. One of her characters was a compulsive Coke drinker, so by the end of the play, she had to go to the bathroom so badly that there would be no possible way she would be able to get through her tap dance solo in the finale without wetting herself. So, she would put on her tap shoes and sprint down the hallways to the ladies' room, changing costumes the entire way, praying that none of the audience would choose that moment to relieve themselves, and taking full advantage of the metal taps that helped her to slide very speedily across the linoleum floors.

Thinking that was the punch line to this particular story, I began to laugh. "No, wait, there's more!" she said, as she began retelling how in the climax scene of the show, she was madly tearing off her clothes for her very last costume change (#24!). To that point, everything had gone flawlessly. That was until one of the backstage crew members told her that he couldn't find the prop she was supposed to take onstage. They began to frantically go through all the clothes and props, because she could not make her entrance without it. As her onstage cue was quickly approaching, they noticed the prop over in a corner. She ran to grab it just in time and managed to make it out there promptly...the only problem was that she had forgotten to put her pants on! In that moment, every actor's recurring nightmare of being on stage in only their underpants had become an embarrassing reality for her!

At first, she had no idea why all the action had stopped, and everyone on stage was staring at her. She thought, *What? I have the prop*. And then she felt a cool breeze across her legs. Unable to contain themselves, her fellow actors burst into laughter, followed by the entire audience. Totally mortified, she made some feeble excuse to scurry off stage only to come back moments later, only this time *with* her pants on.

By now, I was practically falling out of my chair in stitches. I totally connected with her experience! I felt like she was describing a week in my life, and I could relate to the character's role changes all too well, not that I ever have stood anywhere public in just my underpants!

I'm sure you can connect with this story too. As women going for God's "all," when we dissect our lives, the number of different roles we can play on any given day is remarkable: wife, mom, author, sister, friend, neighbor, mentor, spiritual dynamite, employee or a myriad of other roles. Just like this actress, we can race around on the stage of life trying to make sure we've got all our props and costumes worked out for our "audience" and unending "performance."

As I thought about it, I began to realize that more challenging than those costume changes was the fact that she had to keep each of her roles separate and distinct. How was it that she never came on stage in the right scene, but as the wrong character? When I asked her how she did it, she told me something that I believe is a key for us too. She could completely shake off the last character by bringing herself back to the awareness of whom *she* really was—a working actress living in St. Louis—before she moved into the next character. She always remembered to come from that clean perspective of her own identity, and by doing so, she could keep each character unique.

whose role is it, anyway?

Just like this actress, every single one of us has many different roles to fulfill on any given day...and they can change at any given moment! It is little wonder that at times we feel like we are suffering from a multiple personality disorder. We are pulled in so many different directions based on the demands of people around us and their expectations or needs of us. One recent example that typified this was at my mother's 70th birthday party. Within a span of hours, I was characterized by different people in a variety of ways. To one, I was my mom's only daughter, to another I was Nick's wife, to another I was Catherine and Sophia's mom, to another I was George's sister, and to my niece, I was "the cool aunt who buys all the great presents." Some old friends considered me the "weird one" who had "got religion," and conversely, friends from church thought I was a great Bible teacher and author. Okay, I admit, they were totally biased, but clearly very perceptive! And so continued the endless list of identities or roles I apparently had. By the end of the night, I was totally exhausted just thinking about all of the different facets that make me, me.

Whilst it's true that the way each of the partygoers identified me is a legitimate aspect of the various roles I fulfill in life, none of these roles are who I really am. This experience reminded me that people identify us based on what we do (the role we play) rather than who we are. It's often difficult for them to see us as a complete person outside the role in which we relate to them. For instance, I know Sophia can't imagine her mommy as anything else but her mommy, but I know Nick is very happy I don't relate to him only as Sophia's mother.

The only way I'm able to "morph" from role to role and *not* end up mixing them all up is by approaching my life similar to the way my actress friend did during that crazy show. As I wear my many hats throughout any given day, I must make sure I have a constant awareness of who I really am, outside of all the differentthings I do. You see, if I allow all the different roles to define *me* instead of who I truly am in Christ defining *them*, I'm going to get all messed up.

We need to realize that while who we are includes many different roles, not one of them completely defines us. In other words, who you are is not determined by what you do, that is, *your do is not your who*! Add to this the fact that if we try to get our identity, significance and security from what we do, or the roles we play, ultimately our life becomes focused upon mere functionality and doing more, rather than something deeper.

This will likely lead to feelings of frustration, dissatisfaction and emptiness.

So the question we need to ask ourselves is: Who am I *really*? At the end of the day when no one is calling us mommy, wife, sister, mentor, boss or friend, who's left? When all these titles are stripped away, do we still feel valued and confident on the inside, or do we actually feel a little naked, like the actress in her underpants?

The truth is that you can't have and do it all if you don't know who you really are; and who you *really* are can only be found in Christ. Our identity doesn't lie in our gender, ethnicity, socio-economic background, education level or career status. It lies in who we are in Christ.

For me, the issue of what my true identity was hinged on was tested to the core when I was 33 years old and found out, under very shocking circumstances, that I was adopted. The revelation that I was not who I thought I was could have caused me to have a serious breakdown had I not made the choice to focus on who I really was in Christ. I did exactly what my actor friend did to ground herself in between costume changes: I focused on who I really was. The enemy will always challenge our sense of identity, but the best defense (and essential if we are to have and do it all) is fully grasping who we really are in Christ. (I talk about this experience extensively in my book *A Life Unleashed*.) Had I not been firmly rooted in the knowledge of who I really was in Christ, I'm sure I would have completely crumbled. But because I had the Word diligently sown into my heart, I was able to draw on that truth and not be overcome by my circumstances. Day and night, Psalm 139 became my meditation and helped me to keep my head above the water during what was a tumultuous period of my life. I honestly believe that years of grief, anger, resentment, confusion and even therapy were avoided because of the Word and the fact that I knew my true identity, helped me to refocus and see beyond the circumstances.

who am i *really*?

My daughter Catherine knows who she is and has no problem displaying it! She had just started school at the age of five, and one day she had an argument with another little boy from her class. I think it was over a global issue like who was going to take the teddy bear home that night! At one point in the argument, the little boy grabbed the teddy bear from Catherine's arms and said to her, "Catherine Bobbie, you are dumb and ugly." Later that day, Catherine's teacher relayed the story to me because she was stunned by Catherine's response to the situation. She watched as Catherine, having just been insulted, put her shoulders back, looked the little boy squarely in the eyes, and confidently asserted, "No I'm not, my daddy says that I am beautiful and smart." She then proceeded to take the teddy bear back and walk away. I absolutely love this story—not only because my daughter ended up with the teddy bear—but because Catherine displayed the power in knowing what her daddy says about her, which is exactly what your Father in heaven thinks about you! Empowered by knowing what God's Word says about you, you can refute the lies of the enemy when they come.

Just like this little boy, the enemy comes to us on a regular basis, not only to try to snatch away the things in life we want, but also to make us believe we don't even deserve those things! He tells us we are unworthy, unlovable and unable, as he throws insults and doubts at our minds, trying to make us believe we are far less than we really are. But if we can learn to possess the bold, childlike faith of Catherine and simply (and deeply) believe we are who God says we are, then we'll be able to confidently grab that teddy bear right back and walk away with our heads held high. To have and do it all, we must undoubtedly believe we *really* are who God says we are, and we can only achieve this through the Word of God...and *nothing else*!

I encourage you to write down the following Bible verses about who you really are in Christ. Take out your post-it notes. (I'm pretty certain one of the long lost beatitudes of Christ was: *Blessed is the post-it note for it will help reveal great truth.*) Copy these Scriptures, and stick them on every possible surface. Put them on your mirror so you can reflect on them as you're applying lipstick, adhere them to your steering wheel for when you are stuck in traffic (*not* when speeding down the highway!), put them next to your computer at work, stick them right above the toilet paper dispenser for when you are, well...you know, or tape them to the diaper box for when your baby is, well... you know! They will remind you of who your Father in heaven is, what family you belong to, and your true identity—altering your perspective on who you are.

I am a child of God.

But as many as received Him, to them He gave the right to become children of God, to those who believe in His name: who were born, not of blood, nor of the will of the flesh, nor of the will of man, but of God. (John 1:12-13)[1]

I am saved by grace.

For by grace you have been saved through faith, and that not of yourselves; it is the gift of God, not of works, lest anyone should boast. (Ephesians 2:8-9)[2]

I am alive to God and dead to sin.

Likewise you also, reckon yourselves to be dead indeed to sin, but alive to God in Christ Jesus our Lord. (Romans 6:11)[3]

I am sanctified.

For them I sanctify myself, that they too may be truly sanctified. (John 17:19)[4]

I am a new creation.

Therefore, if anyone is in Christ, he is a new creation, the old has gone, the new has come! (2 Corinthians 5:17)[5]

I am a royal daughter.

But you are a chosen people, a royal priesthood, a holy nation, a people belonging to God, that you may declare the praises of him who called you out of darkness into his wonderful light. (1 Peter 2:9)[6]

I am reconciled to God.

That God was reconciling the world to Himself in Christ, not counting men's sins against them. And He has committed to us the message of reconciliation. (2 Corinthians 5:19)[7]

I am free.

Therefore if the Son makes you free, you shall be free indeed. (John 8:36)[8]

I am justified.

Know that a man is not justified by observing the law, but by faith in Jesus Christ. So we, too, have put our faith in Christ Jesus that we may be justified by faith in Christ and not by observing the law, because by observing the law no one will be justified. (Galatians 2:16)[9]

I am chosen.

For He chose us in Him before the creation of the world to be holy and blameless in His sight (Ephesians 1:4)[10]

I am adopted.

Having predestined us to adoption as sons by Jesus Christ to Himself, according to the good pleasure of His will. (Ephesians 1:5)[11]

I am accepted.

To the praise of the glory of His grace, by which He made us accepted in the Beloved. (Ephesians 1:6)[12]

I am forgiven.

And be kind to one another, tenderhearted, forgiving one another, even as God in Christ forgave you. (Ephesians 4:32)[13]

I am predestined.

In Him also we have obtained an inheritance, being predestined according to the purpose of Him who works all things according to the counsel of His will. (Ephesians 1:11)[14]

I am raised and seated in heavenly realms.

Raised us up together, and made us sit together in the heavenly places in Christ Jesus. (Ephesians 2:6)[15]

I am created for good works.

For we are His workmanship, created in Christ Jesus for good works, which God prepared beforehand that we should walk in them. (Ephesians 2:10)[16]

I am called to eternal glory.

But may the God of all grace, who called us to His eternal glory by Christ Jesus, after you have suffered a while, perfect, establish, strengthen, and settle you. (1 Peter 5:10)[17]

I am more than a conqueror.

Yet in all these things we are more than conquerors through Him who loved us. (Romans 8:37)[18]

I am an overcomer.

These things I have spoken to you, that in Me you may have peace. In the world you will have tribulation; but be of good cheer, I have overcome the world. (John 16:33)[19]

I am never forsaken.

For He [God] Himself has said, I will not in any way fail you nor give you up nor leave you without support. [I will] not, [I will] not, [I will] not in any degree leave you helpless nor forsake nor let [you] down (relax My hold on you)! [Assuredly not!] (Hebrews 13:5)[20]

I am the righteousness of God in Christ.

This righteousness from God comes through faith in Jesus Christ to all who believe. (Romans 3:22)[21]

Girls, without truly knowing who we are in Him, we will always struggle, attempting to gain our identity from "having and doing it all," as opposed to getting our identity from Christ.

identity theft

Knowing our true identity is only half the battle; once we know it, we have to guard it. I recently received a distraught call from my friend, Alex, who told me that someone had taken her checking account number and created and used checks with her information. She had become the victim of identity theft: the fastest growing crime in the USA.

In the weeks following, Alex encountered nothing but frustration as she couldn't use her credit cards, draw money from the bank, or travel until she was able to prove that she was who she said she was. It hindered every aspect of her life until it was finally cleared up weeks later. Her life ceased to function effectively or move forward whilst she had no "identity."

As a result of this experience, Alex has gone to great lengths to stop it from ever happening again by protecting any information that could make her susceptible. She has new passwords on her accounts, she no longer has phone numbers on her checks, she never gives her credit card details on the Internet unless it's a secure site, she is super careful at ATMs and she is sure to shred or safely file all important documents. This might sound like a case of paranoia, but in fact, she is just taking all necessary precautions to protect her identity.

In the same way, it is crucial we do all that we can to ensure we protect our identity in Christ. The Bible teaches us, *"The thief does not come except to steal, and to kill, and to destroy."*[22] That's why it's so important to follow through with those post-it notes! It's one thing to have a list of all of these Scriptures, but quite another to actually know them in your heart of hearts, ready to use during times of challenge and crisis. If we're not careful to take the steps designed to protect our blood-bought identities, then while we're busily trying to forge our identities by having and doing it all, we run the risk of the enemy stealing our true identity from us.

While it is true that the enemy comes to steal, kill and destroy, he can only take from us what we allow him to take. If we're confident about who we are in Christ, then nothing and no one can rob us of that. If our confidence is based on the wrong thing, we can often be left floundering and no longer pursuing God's "all" for our life when our circumstances change.

Let me attempt to explain what happens here in a little more detail. In our journey of having and doing it all, we can lose ourselves somewhere along the way in one particular role. For some, it's being a great mom, but when our kids grow up and move out, we feel as if we no longer know our role in life, or even who we are. For others, we are driven and ambitious career women, but an unexpected company changeover could quickly rob us of our title, or more importantly, our identity, if that is where we have placed it. It is all too easy to find our identity in being a certain role, instead of being in Christ. The moment our "do" becomes our "who," we end up trapped in that one role and begin hindering the "all" God had for us. This is a pattern that can happen in any season of life, so we need to stay alert!

Perhaps we've gained our sense of identity, significance and security from our physical looks or from the designer labels. Then we start to age, and parts of our body begin to migrate to the Deep South. (National Geographic boobs, anyone?) An identity crisis sets in because we no longer know who we are without the perfect body, or without the most expensive clothes. Our eyes have gotten away from Jesus, and we began to find our sense of self in the wrong things. When our identity is secure in Christ, we know we are daughters of the King, regardless of our body shape or what we wear.

In the same way we go to great measures to protect our credit cards, our Internet banking details, our private accounts and our personal documents, let's also ensure that in our pursuit of having and doing it all, we do not lose the solid foundation which is our true identity, that is, who we are in Christ (which is unchanging).

This fight for our identity is a huge one; perhaps the one we women struggle with above everything else. Sister, wife, mother, friend, boss, mentor, leader, aunt: as long as you're breathing, you will constantly be operating in a variety of roles. At times, we can take our eyes off of who we really are through Jesus Christ and look instead to our function, title or what we do. If prolonged, a major identity crisis is likely somewhere along the road of life.

Let's avoid that whole drama, and instead approach our having and doing it all like the actress at the beginning of this chapter. Let's take the time to stop for a moment, focus on God's voice, and remind ourselves who we *really* are; otherwise, we'll find ourselves so caught up in the whirlwind of role morphing that we will inevitably walk out the door in only our underpants!

it's all about simplicity

chapter five
it's all about simplicity

Even if I tried, I don't think I could tell you the number of times I've found myself in an airport. Calculating how often I have been through the process of ticketing, security, boarding and clearing customs would be nearly impossible. However, few of my traveling journeys were as frustrating as this particular one. It was early morning and I had 30 hours of flying time and two layovers ahead of me; but I had a nice, warm Starbucks coffee in my hand, so despite the early rising, life was good. Ticketing and bag checking went seamlessly and I was off to security. That's when everything started to spiral downward. The security line was unusually long, but I'm a patient gal (plus I had my Starbucks) so this was not too big of a deal; but as I got closer to the front of the line, I could hear a general grumbling coming from the travelers ahead of me. A guy in front of me said something about new security regulations. I didn't think anything of it because, like I said, I'd been through this process a zillion times.

I smiled as I took my shoes off, hoping to be a happy light to the grumpy folks around me. And then I was stopped by one of the security guards. Actually, it was me who came to an abrupt stop because he reached for my Starbucks! Luckily, I pulled my cup back before he got his paws on the hot nectar from the heavens. I was about to say, *"I prefer not to share my coffee with strangers,"* when he told me I had to dump it before going through security. *What?!* I thought. *Throw away an unfinished Starbucks?* Now that was a difficult concept to wrap my mind around! Before I could protest too loudly, he explained there were a few new safety guidelines, and not taking liquids beyond security was one of them.

My choices: drink it all, and quick, or dump it. I began to weigh my options: *I can't possibly go through this morning without my caffeine and that airplane coffee is like drinking a liquid ashtray... but it's still way too hot to guzzle.* I decided a burnt tongue would do me no good as I had to speak at a conference immediately following my arrival, so reluctantly, I dropped the cup into the large trash can. I'd like to say I was able to manage a smile at the "coffee police," but I'm quite certain it looked more like a snarl as I walked by.

I went through the metal detector and quickly grabbed my shoes, hoping to have the time to find another Starbucks before my plane started to board. As if having smelled the urgency in my actions, a different security person took my carry-on luggage and asked me to follow him to the security table so he could go through my belongings. Before I could respond, he had my bag open and was sifting through the contents. Holding up a container of hairspray somewhat disapprovingly, he said, "Sorry, ma'am, this can't go through." And with no negotiation; *bam!* It was gone, tossed in the trash along with the belongings of many other unsuspecting travelers.

A little stunned, I thought to myself, *Alright, so maybe I can do without my Starbucks, but I can't go onstage after 30 hours of traveling without hairspray! Does this guy not see how flat my hair is right now? If this was a **female** security person, I'm sure she would understand my predicament!* Then, I saw him reach for my hand lotion. *Please, not the lotion! My hands get so dry during a long flight; I absolutely can't survive without it. **Bam!*** There went another item into the great abyss! Then the unthinkable happened. He pulled out my one-and-only, no-other-color-has-ever-made-me-look-this-ravishing tube of lipstick. He couldn't be serious. Suddenly, the situation went into slow motion as I saw the precious lip color fall through his fingers and begin tumbling toward the mouth of the trashcan. "Noooooooooooooo!" I said as I lunged to save the lipstick, but I was too late. *Baaaaammmm!* It had disappeared into the trash. "Sorry, ma'am. No can do," he said matter-of-factly as he zipped up my bag, handed it to me and walked away.

The encounter had successfully transformed me from nice Christine into cranky Christine! Wondering how I was going to make up for those lost items, I trudged to my gate, but little did I know that the scaling back had just begun. After 30 hours of flying, I arrived in Norway with just enough time to pick up my bags before driving to the conference. The only problem was that my suitcases had decided to take a different route! There I stood in my tracksuit and tennis shoes, an hour away from having to walk on stage to speak to hundreds of people with no hairspray, no lipstick, no lotion and no change of clothes! I thought to myself, *it's bad enough to go up there as flat-haired, flaky-handed and pale-lipped, but I simply cannot go up there wearing this tracksuit!*

At that point however, I had no other option. I put aside my vanity and went and preached my heart out. I have to admit that once I got into the flow, I completely forgot about my hair, my makeup and my clothes, and it was not until after the altar call, as many people were coming forward to receive Jesus, that I remembered how concerned I had been about all that stuff. The thought struck me, *while I'd rather have been on the platform in a freshly pressed set of clothes and my favorite lip color, I certainly didn't* **need** *any of it to get the job done. God still did everything He was going to do, and His anointing on the message was not proportional to the puffiness of my hair.* I learned a great lesson that day: I can live with so much less than I think I can! Sure, it's nice to have "the stuff" when it's available, but it's amazing how some things we can think are so essential, really aren't that important.

the art of simplification

If we're to have and do it all, we need to master the art of simplifying our lives. When Jesus began his ministry here on earth, he brought a message of life, liberty *and* simplification to people who were bound by the complexity of over-demanding

laws and regulations. The Jewish law, which originally con-
sisted of the 10 simple commandments given to Moses, had
evolved into a list of 613 commandments by the time Jesus
walked the earth. Can you imagine going through each day
trying to obey (let alone remember) 613 laws about every detail of your life? There were strict rules about how to clean
certain dishes, how to wash your hands, how to eat your food,
how to deal in business, how to tithe to God, how to interact
in society and the list goes on. I wouldn't have been able to
make it out of my door every morning without breaking at
least 18 of them.

Jesus felt compassion for people who were bound by these unnecessary yokes and burdens of religion because God never
intended such complexity for our lives. In fact, in a single exchange with the Pharisees, He simplified the 613 Mosaic laws
down into just two. *"'You shall love the Lord your God with all your
heart, with all your soul, and with all your mind.' This is the first and
great commandment. And the second is like it: 'You shall love your
neighbor as yourself.' On these two commandments hang all the Law
and the Prophets."[1]*

Can you believe Jesus said that *all* of the law and the prophets hung on just two commandments? For those of us who
struggle with mathematics, let me make this as clear as possible. In three verses of Scripture, 613 laws became two. Now
that is simplification at its best!

Trust me, I understand how difficult this sounds because,
by nature, I'm a very complex person. I love to analyze...
well, *everything*! People, situations, conversations, spiritual

concepts—you name it, I've analyzed it. And then after I've completed my analysis, I feel the need to reanalyze the post-analysis of my pre-analysis! Nick laughs at me because he can't comprehend how (or why) any person would choose to dissect anything on as many levels as I do. He gets exhausted just trying to follow one pathway of my intricate multi-dimensional web of analysis.

The truth is, we women sometimes have a tendency to make things so complicated! We can put unnecessary pressure on ourselves to achieve and do so much more than God asks or even expects from us. This often results in feelings of inadequacy, stress, anxiety and being stuck on a self imposed performance treadmill. Subsequently, our lives are full of activity, but with little forward motion or progress. Inevitably, our friends, families, colleagues and often God, bear the brunt of our overcommitted lifestyles. No wonder we feel overwhelmed; we were not meant to do life like this.

A life of having and doing it all should not be burdensome or full of stress and anxiety, and we must learn to find rest in Christ. Jesus clearly articulates this when He says:

> *"Come to Me, all you who labor and are heavy-laden and overburdened, and I will cause you to rest. [I will ease and relieve and refresh your souls.] Take My yoke upon you and learn of Me, for I am gentle (meek) and humble (lowly) in heart, and you will find rest (relief and ease and refreshment and recreation and blessed quiet) for your souls. For My yoke is wholesome (useful, good--not harsh, hard, sharp,*

or pressing, but comfortable, gracious, and pleasant), and
My burden is light and easy to be borne."[2]

What this Scripture makes clear for me is that our "all" is inseparable from His yoke and burden. Let me explain it this way: firstly, for the uninitiated, a yoke is a wooden beam that connects two animals such as oxen to assist with pulling a load, and it also refers to a length of wood carried over the shoulders to balance two equal weights. Now imagine a person who has a yoke on their shoulders carrying two buckets, one on each end of the yoke. The yoke provides for a more even distribution or redistribution of the weight of the buckets, which in turn enables the person to carry the buckets of water longer, farther and with greater ease than if they had carried the buckets by hand. By using the yoke, they will be able to go beyond their own natural limitations.

Now back to Jesus. When we are wearing His yoke, the stress and the pressure we sometimes feel as we try to have and do it all dissipates. Don't get me wrong, we still have to do the hard work and pull our weight, but it's not so heavy that it will kill us. Why? Because as we exchange our yoke and burden for Jesus', we no longer carry the weight of everything in our own strength. What a relief! Remember, "Superwoman" is a media myth, so take the pressure off and go after being a *supernatural* woman. She can have and do God's "all" because she has put on the yoke and carried the burden of Christ, not her own.

it's time to simplify

I'm sure you've experienced that frustrating moment when you've arrived at the checkout counter, glad to have made it through the grocery store alive (especially the kids), reached into your purse to pay, but it's so full that you can't even find your wallet. You begin to frantically dump the entire contents of the bag onto the counter only to discover antiquities almost dating back to the Dark Ages—half-eaten mints, movie stubs from last year, a pacifier (and your youngest just turned 13), that earring you've been looking for and enough coins to buy your next car. Sometimes our lives can look just like an overstuffed handbag. We find ourselves carrying so many needless weights and burdens. And just like all the unnecessary contents in our purses can keep us from finding our wallets, these internal weights and burdens will hinder us from having and doing it all. Solution? It's time to simplify!

But in an age of lightning fast technology, worldwide interconnectedness, mass media saturation, endless noise and a culture of over-programmed schedules, unless we *intentionally* take steps to simplify our lives, it's never going to happen; we're never going to lose the weights. I know, I know—like you wanted to become aware of another kind of weight problem!

Seriously though, what woman at some point of her life has not been obsessed with losing weight? Low carb, all carb, or supplements made of genetically engineered fat melting flowers grown on Mars, you name it, it's likely we've either heard about it, read about it or tried it! Drawing a spiritual truth from a physical one—whilst it might feel great to fit back into your skinny jeans, we cannot just stop there. Spiritually speaking, ladies, it's time to lose "weight" in this realm as well! The Bible makes it clear that we all need to strip off every weight that would slow us down and hinder us from having and doing it all.

Hebrews 12:1-2 says, *"Therefore, since we are surrounded by such a huge crowd of witnesses to the life of faith, let us **strip off every weight that slows us down**, especially the sin that so easily trips us up. And let us run with endurance the race God has set before us. We do this by keeping our eyes on Jesus, the champion who initiates and perfects our faith."*[3]

I think some of the weights that the writer to the Hebrews is referring to are the internal ones. Things like jealousy, comparison, anger, worry, anxiety, fear, insecurity, unforgiveness, bitterness, offence, lust, greed, envy...and the list goes on.

Every one of us needs to do a regular inventory of every area of our life in order to identify and drop any unnecessary baggage we've inevitably picked up along the way. In the same way those extra pounds can begin to creep on when we're not conscious of eating right and exercising regularly, so it is with our internal world. Just as I go to the gym regularly to maintain my fitness, there are also five things I intentionally do on a regular basis to ensure my spiritual fitness.

Breathe

Busy, busy, busy...we are always so busy. Busy for eight hours compulsively cleaning every corner of the house, or busy gossiping on the phone with friends, or busy completing every single task at the office before day's end (even though many of them could wait), or busy ironing our socks so they will perfectly fit in our color coordinated sock drawer. Many of us are driven by the urgency of our schedules because we have wasted so much time on relatively purposeless activity. We need to evaluate: *what things in my life can I replace with time for me in order to recharge and breathe?*

I have found that the greatest gift I can give to Nick and the girls is a healthy me, and the only way I am able to be the best me is if I have taken the time to recharge my soul and spirit. If I allow all of my personal time to be eaten up by activities that do not enrich or inspire me, then it's not long before I'm feeling frazzled. I have to be very disciplined to actually set aside time for just me, and use that precious time wisely!

For some, this looks like sitting in a comfy chair, sipping a coffee and reading a good book; for others, it's putting on the running shoes and going for a jog in the park. It can be listening to inspirational music, or gardening, or cooking, or simply sitting on the porch watching the sunset. It's crucial not to allow our *having* and *doing* to consume us so much that we get to a place where we have no space in our schedules to recharge and regroup.

An essential by-product of stopping to breathe and stilling our spirit and mind is that it gives God time to get a word in edgewise and speak to us! Psalm 23:1-3 says, *"The Lord is my shepherd; I shall not want. He makes me to lie down in green pastures; He leads me beside the still waters. He restores my soul; He leads me in the paths of righteousness for His name's sake."[4]* So much of our mental confusion, emotional outbursts and physical exhaustion would greatly dissipate if we would simply take the time to stop, breathe and lean into the presence of God.

Learn to Say "No"

I have discovered that "no" is often one of the most difficult words to say. Women are basically wired to think of themselves last. We want to make everyone else happy which can cause us to neglect ourselves in the process. We can end up feeling like we're scraping the bottom of the emotional barrel, but it's not necessarily because everyone else has taken advantage of us; more often than not it's because we haven't mastered the art of saying "no". If we're to have and do it all, knowing when to say "no" is as equally important as learning when to say "yes."

In my own life, this has been a great challenge for many different reasons. Apart from the fact that by nature I love to be involved in everything, in the early days of my Christian walk, I was still wounded and broken because of the abuse I experienced in my past. I had lived with rejection, abandonment, guilt, shame and unforgiveness. In an attempt to feel loved, valued and accepted, I never wanted to disappoint people so I inadvertently became a people-pleaser, craving the approval of man at times above the approval of God. One way this was outworked in my life was that I accepted every ministry invitation, not wanting to disappoint anyone, regardless of the toll this took on my body and my relationships. Another was that I felt I had to personally help every person who had been wounded or broken, and so I accepted an unhealthy amount of counseling appointments. Obviously this was not a sustainable way of life or ministry, as you can't please all of the people all of the time. I ended each day feeling depleted, emptied out and exhausted. Everything I was doing was good and helpful to people, but the problem was that I was saying yes to many of these things from an underlying need for approval and acceptance, instead of from a position of strength and wholeness.

As I've already shared in earlier chapters of this book, in order to have and do it all, it is imperative that we find our identity in Christ. Paul summed this up when he wrote, *"Obviously, I'm not trying to win the approval of people, but of God. If pleasing people were my goal, I would not be Christ's servant."*[5]

This pattern of constant activity and striving continued until I accepted personal responsibility for my choices and embarked on the difficult journey of dealing with my own brokenness. I knew that instead of being a wounded healer, I needed to establish healthy boundaries and learn to say "no" to others (and myself) so I could say "yes" to God.

For many, this "yes" addiction can be much more subtle. For instance, if you have a house full of teenagers and all of them are involved in every imaginable sporting or extra-curricular activity, it won't be long before your house feels like utter chaos. Some of us have kids with so many commitments that we need to hire a personal assistant simply to navigate the family through the complex maze of everyone's schedules! It is very important for all of us to stop and ask the questions: *Is all of this activity molding my kids into healthy Christians? Which of these activities are sharpening their true gifts and talents?* In order to maintain having and doing it all in the family realm, and in our lives more generally, we must learn to simplify!

Be Yourself

Have you ever been shopping and found an outfit that looks identical to the one your favorite celebrity wore on the red carpet, and for a fraction of the price? So you buy it only to realize it doesn't quite look like it did on the waif-thin actress. The clothes don't feel right and you don't quite feel like yourself in them. It's probably because, while the outfit looks great on the celebrity, it's not your style! I can't tell you how many times I've wanted to buy something, but after trying the "look" on in the dressing room, I quickly discover this 5'2" Greek woman simply can't pull it off!

Way too often, we women get so caught up with trying to be like someone else we forget how special we are (That's why the first four chapters of this book are so crucial in our quest to have and do it all). Galatians 6:4 says, *"Each of you should test your own actions. Then you can take pride in yourself, without comparing yourself to somebody else."*[6] Comparing your life, your calling, your schedule or even your way of doing things with someone else's will only bring frustration.

For instance, my neighbor is a brilliant stay-at-home-mom raising several children, an effective member of the PTA, a freelance graphic artist who volunteers this gift once a week at her church—and still is able to cook a gourmet meal each night for her family. What if she looked over her fence into my life and decided that having and doing it all meant she needed to do all the things she's wired to do *and* everything she saw me doing...even though she absolutely hates traveling and public speaking? Now, that would be a problem! Her husband and kids would be frustrated that she was gone so much pursuing something she doesn't even enjoy; plus she'd eventually get kicked off the PTA for too many absentee votes, and her church would be forced to revert back to using clip art. And I don't even want to think about the chaos my family would experience if I tried to accomplish her "all," while simultaneously traveling and preaching around the world and helping victims of human trafficking. Clearly, we should each pursue having and doing our own unique "all." So relax...love yourself and who God made you to be. Life's so much simpler when you do!

Trust God

We girls love security. We want to know who we're going to marry, how many children we're going to have, whether or not our husbands will get that promotion at work...then we want to know who our kids are going to marry and how many children *they're* going to have! From the time we wake up until the moment our heads hit the pillow at night, there are countless issues we could choose to worry about. But do you know what I have found to be true? Almost nothing that I've allowed to consume me and make me anxious has ever come to fruition. And even if it has, God has always showed Himself to be much bigger than the situation.

I can't recount the amount of sleep I've lost worrying about things I ultimately couldn't control anyway. I had to discipline myself to intentionally *"be anxious for nothing, but in everything by prayer and supplication, with thanksgiving, let your requests be made known to God; and the peace of God, which surpasses all understanding, will guard your hearts and minds through Christ Jesus."*[7] Often we do not have and do it all because we are filled with anxiety and have no room left to have and do God's "all."

I have had to learn to substitute my anxiety with God's peace and this could ultimately only be achieved through prayer. I believe there's a direct correlation between our trusting God and our prayer life. Prayer is our way to communicate with our Father and an opportunity for us to bring our gratitude, needs and concerns before Him. Sometimes we feel that we may not have enough time to pray because, *Oh my gosh, I have a zillion things to do today: drop the kids off at school, finish the paperwork that was due yesterday, pick up the dry-cleaning, arrange dinner for my family so they don't die of starvation...as if I possibly have time to pray!* Believe me, I completely understand how it feels to be pulled in so many directions (which is precisely why I'm writing this book!), and convince myself that I just didn't have the extra slot in my day to pray. I was not able to find the peace in my heart about my prayer life until I discovered this one thing: prayer has no formal location or time-slot requirement! Simply put, prayer is a way of life.

When Paul says in 1 Thessalonians that we should *"pray without ceasing,"*[8] he was obviously not suggesting we should be in a head-bowed, eyes-closed posture all day long. What Paul was referring to is an *attitude* of God-consciousness and God-surrender that we carry with us all the time. When we pray, we are trusting God with our needs and future, rather than depending on ourselves. In essence, unceasing prayer means continual dependence upon and constant communion with our Father, and with this comes the supernatural peace that only God can give. Whenever an issue comes up in your day, no matter how big or how small, stop for a moment and talk to God about it. Learn to run to Him in prayer *first*.

Let Go of the Past

We've already established my obsession with purging my house, office, car and any other space I might occupy from needless junk and clutter. In the same way, we have to get good at "purging" the things from our past that can limit us or hold us back. In fact, Paul said, *"Not that I have already attained, or am already perfected; but I press on, that I may lay hold of that for which Christ Jesus has also laid hold of me. Brethren, I do not count myself to have apprehended; but one thing I do, forgetting those things which are behind and reaching forward to those things which are ahead, I press toward the goal for the prize of the upward call of God in Christ Jesus."*[9]

You can't embrace all that is in your future whilst holding on to all that is in your past. If we spend our time rehashing and replaying every scenario from our past where someone hurt us, abused us, disappointed us or where we have failed, then we will never be able to reach forward to grasp the future God has prepared for us. Sometimes we hang on very tightly to past memories, feelings, or experiences as if they are happening in the present, and as a result, we end up missing out on our "all" for now because of our attachment to the past.

It takes courage to simplify our lives and to let go of the weights we have been holding onto for years. Whether those are actual, physical things in which we find our identity like clothes, cars, jewelry or houses, or less tangible weights like relationships, bad habits, wrong thinking or emotional baggage, we need to rid ourselves of them if we are going to have and do it all. Even me, the Queen of Purging, can fall into the trap at times of holding on to things a little too tightly: ways of thinking or patterns of behavior that can begin to weigh me down. Therefore, in order to continue to pursue the God-adventure for my life, I must constantly follow the prompting of the Holy Spirit to simplify and eradicate the excess weights. Remember, so much of what we can think is absolutely essential for fulfilling our destiny just isn't that important! Girls, let the simplification begin!

it's all about seasons

chapter six
it's all about seasons

What is that deafening sound, and why is it going off so early in the morning? I tried to stuff my head beneath my pillow to drown it out, but it was of no use. I reached for a second pillow, hoping the old adage, *two are better than one,* held truth. It actually worked, but it was only a few minutes before I realized I was going to have to choose between the awful sound of the alarm clock or suffocation. I made the painful decision to get up, find out whose alarm was going off at this ridiculous hour, beat them senseless with my pillow, unplug their clock and then snuggle back into bed for a few more hours of shut-eye. As I unearthed myself from the mountain of pillows, it dawned on me that the source of the alarm was...*my* alarm!

Why did I set an alarm? Isn't this my day off? I thought. It was then that I remembered I had signed up to help clean the church. For about a minute, I tried to justify why I should call and cancel, but as the fuzziness in my head began to wear off, I knew I would never be able to enjoy my day knowing I had gone back on my word. *Once I get a cup of coffee in me, I'll be raring to go.* And then I tripped out of bed. *Okay, maybe two cups of coffee!*

As I drove to the church, I wondered why in the world I felt so compelled to spend my only day off scrubbing toilets. *I didn't realize that when I said "yes" to ministry, and a life of coming boldly into the throne room, God was referring to this kind of throne!* (That thought made me chuckle. The caffeine was obviously beginning to kick in.) *But seriously God, when are you going to give me a chance to sink my teeth into some **real** ministry opportunity?* No answer from heaven...maybe God was still on His first cup, too!

When I got to the church, there were no other volunteers in sight. Undeterred, I headed to the supply cupboard. *I might as well start with the hardest tasks first so I can check those off right away,* I thought. So I grabbed the toilet brushes and headed for the men's restroom. *Certainly, no one expects me to go near the urinals!* Just the thought of it made me gag a little. I offered up a small prayer for the inventor of the latex glove and took my first steps into the man-cave. It was at that rather inopportune moment that I bumped into the assistant youth pastor, John. "Whoa! Aren't you going into the wrong bathroom?" he asked, not noticing the toilet brush in my hand. Before I could explain, he said:

"Hey, you're Christine, right? Aren't you the one with the degree in psychology?" Before I could answer him that it was actually English History, he blurted, "How would you like to work in a youth center?"

"What's a youth center?" I replied.

"I don't really know, but we just got awarded a government grant to run a youth center. The only problem is, I'm going on a missions trip for the next month, and I can't work on it right now. But I need to have a youth center by the time I get back. Can you take it for me?"

I wanted to say that I had only come this morning to clean some bathrooms (why all of a sudden I felt the urge to defend my toilet ministry was beyond me), so instead I just stared at him. He must have taken my silence as agreement because he tossed a pager at me as he darted out of the church and shouted over his shoulder, "Thanks, Christine! Call me if you need anything."

What just happened? I thought, toilet brush at my feet, having dropped out of my hand so I could catch the pager. *What did he mean by all that youth center stuff? I haven't the slightest idea how or what to do!* I quickly realized I wouldn't be doing too much scrubbing that day.

I figured the least I could do was learn how to use the pager. It wasn't long before I discovered the pager *was* the youth center! It was 1990 and this popular device was the virtual office. A person would call an "office" number, a receptionist would field the call, tell the caller you were currently unavailable then forward the person's name and number to your pager. You would then race to the nearest phone (remember life before cell phones?) and call them back.

What little I did know about youth centers (which wasn't much at all) was that a pager does not maketh a youth center. However, I had no clue where to go from there. While I had a desire to change the world for Jesus, I had no real inclination of becoming too involved with youth ministry. But there I stood with a pager in hand, and a pastor was going to be back in a month to see what I did with it.

Over the coming days, I visited all the youth centers in our city and found myself getting excited about the possibilities. I began to see how we could effectively reach, impact and help "at risk" young people through the provision of different services. Next, I pulled together a small team of volunteers so we could accomplish more. We began writing and mailing submissions and proposals—all the while having no real idea what we were doing—and within two weeks we received a letter from an organization willing to donate a facility along with some furniture and fresh paint! We were stunned! People and volunteers started gathering around the cause, and over the next several months, the project exploded and it wasn't long before our youth center was thriving.

To be perfectly honest, no one was more surprised than me at the growth and favor we were experiencing. While going through Bible college, I'd never had the internal desire to speak to teenagers in our local community, but rather had a dream to travel the globe and minister to people in different nations and see them come to Christ. However, the fact was, on that fateful day when I showed up to scrub toilets, someone had thrown a pager, and I was the only one who "happened" to be there to catch it. I had prayed a simple prayer, *God I will do whatever*, and it came in the form of a pager and the fledgling notion of pioneering a youth center in our city.

As a 23-year old, there was no possible way I could have imagined how much of my future hinged on how I responded to that moment. Imagine if I had thrown the pager right back to Pastor John, explaining that I didn't feel like God's call on my life was to work with teenagers. Or out of duty, half-heartedly done a few things for the youth center, all the while waiting for my "real" destiny to kick in (as if destinies just "kick in"). But in my heart, I knew God wanted me to take ownership of the task He had placed before me. If I could only be faithful with what was in my hand, then God would one day give me the desires of my heart.

Looking back, I truly believe it was my receptive and obedient spirit that helped launch me into one of the most defining and stretching seasons of my life—one that internally prepared and equipped me for so many of the seasons that have followed. I can now clearly see how that day was actually a God-ordained opportunity.

"all" doesn't mean "all at once"

In having and doing it all, we must realize that God strategically gives us our "all" in layers, in seasons, each one according to *His* perfect timeframe which, by the way, usually takes a lot longer than we want!

This can be frustrating because we would love for our "all" to just drop out of the sky and into our laps...*today*! We've seen a glimpse of our "all" and we want to be living in it right now. Rather than appreciating every part of our life as a God-given season of preparation and molding, we can grow impatient and dissatisfied, especially when that particular season feels mundane, difficult, frustrating or everlasting. The truth is that every single season—school, singlehood, career, marriage, motherhood, even those that involve toilet brushes—is a gift from God. It's not a *means to our "all,"* but rather *part* of it. That means every single one of us is living in a slice of our *"all"* at this very moment. When we grasp this thought, it will not only enable us to see the opportunities for learning and growth in this season, but also help us to embrace the exciting things that are going on right now. We need to learn to love the season we're in whilst simultaneously keeping a fresh and expectant attitude about all that lies ahead.

King Solomon, writing in Ecclesiastes was very aware of the importance of seasons and making the most of each. He wrote: *"For everything there is a season, a time for every activity under heaven."*[1]

I know it certainly doesn't feel like a gift when we're changing our 14th poop-filled diaper of the day, or when we've tediously been finishing those term papers and studying for exams, or when we're working our tails off at an entry-level job, or attending yet another wedding, feeling like we are the only single person left on planet. It's very easy to become discouraged and forget we're actually moving forward in our destiny. We begin to think, *Is all this stuff I am doing really getting me anywhere in life?* We wonder if we somehow slipped off God's radar and are stuck doing laps in a proverbial desert.

I have definitely had seasons when I felt like I was in the back end of a desert somewhere, wondering when I'd ever get the opportunity to travel and tell people about Jesus. In those times it seemed as if what was in my heart was never going to happen. And maybe that's exactly how you feel right now: in the middle of a desert, waiting for God to do something. Let me reassure you—God is so faithful to bring to fulfillment the dreams He has placed in your heart!

So much of our quest to have and do it all relies on whether or not we're actually *prepared* to have and do it all. There are constant moments of preparation in every day of every season. We can't allow ourselves to get so focused on where we want to be that we overlook the wonderful things God is trying to do through us in the present.

The reason I know this is because it's *exactly* how I felt that day I was on my way to the church to clean toilets. I kept asking myself why I was volunteering all of my free time to wipe down bathroom sinks when my true passion was preaching the Gospel and seeing people all over the world come to know Jesus. I had this definite inner sense that God had called me into this type of full-time ministry and that cleaning toilets did not factor into my calling. Shouldn't I be at home reading my Bible and planning my future sermons? Maybe standing on my bed using a brush (*not* of the toilet variety!) for a microphone and practicing my altar calls? But you see, it's in the seemingly insignificant and mundane moments of life that *we* feel are amounting to nothing that *God* is using to get us ready for the next season.

every season matters

I wonder if Moses ever thought of giving up. He's a perfect example of how God uses every season to prepare us for our biggest moments; at least, if we will let Him. Moses was a Hebrew baby who was adopted by the Egyptian Pharaoh's daughter. (You can read all of the details of his life starting in Exodus 2.) The first 40 years of his life were spent in Pharaoh's palace, where he was educated by the finest teachers and trained for leadership by the best in the land. Then, an inner call stirred him to help his people who had been living in the bondage of slavery to the Egyptians for over 400 years. But rather than wait for his opportunity, Moses took his destiny into his own hands. One day, he saw an Egyptian mercilessly beating a Hebrew slave. Moses' anger flared, and as retribution, he killed the Egyptian and hid his body in the sand. When Pharaoh heard of his crime, he sought to kill Moses, but Moses fled into the desert to the land of Midian, where he married, had children, became a shepherd and remained for four long decades; that is, until God showed up in the burning bush.

Moses spent 14,600 days in the backside of a desert. *Fourteen thousand, six hundred days!* There *had* to have been at least a few occasions when, sitting on a rock, sand in his sandals, watching over his flock, he must have wondered, *How in the world did I wind up here?* Moses could have devalued that season and written off all those days as meaningless. Although the Bible doesn't say much about what Moses did during those 40 years, it's clear he spent the season honoring God because when God "suddenly" showed up on day 14,601 in a burning bush, Moses was ready to respond, and in so doing, changed the course of history for the then-known world! What if Moses had given up? The people of Israel would have remained oppressed, perhaps for generations, until God could raise up another person to complete the task destined for Moses.

To have and do it all, we must realize that it is often in the desert of anonymity and obscurity that God molds and shapes our characters, making us ready on the inside for all He has for us. Unfortunately it's also during these times of waiting and preparation that we are most vulnerable to growing weary and giving up on having and doing God's "all." The enemy tries to convince us that our dreams for extraordinary living are not worth the wait, too difficult, or even impossible to achieve. As a result, we can settle for a mediocre, desert-dwelling existence. We can end up thinking: *What's the use of staying pure until I'm married if I'm past my prime before I find my husband? What difference does it make if I cheat a tiny bit on my job when nobody is watching? So what if I treat my husband and kids second-rate today; it's not like that is going to alter my destiny.*

Don't allow yourself to get lost in the seasons of life, or to devalue today—God is using it to prepare you for your tomorrow.

staying focused

I love summer. As a little girl, I couldn't wait for summer to come, and at the first hint of a warm breeze, I'd start begging my mom to take me swimming, trying to convince her it was finally warm enough. She'd chuckle at me standing before her while she pointed out all the goose bumps on my arms and legs. "Christine, if it's so warm outside, what are those?"

Finally, summer would come and I'd savor each moment; so much so that I would try to stay in "summer mode" for as long as possible. But it was all over once Mom could see my breath in the air as I played on the porch before school. Out came the coats and scarves, and away went the sandals and swimmers. And I'd begin counting down the sleeps until the *next* summer.

I wonder how much I missed as I desperately awaited the arrival of my favorite season or as I tried to hang on to it for as long as possible? I wonder how many of us do a similar thing during the different seasons we journey through?

If we are constantly looking forward to what is to come, or reminiscing on the events of seasons past, we will never live in the now! Here are some tips that have helped keep me focused on today—on the now—and not get caught in the trap of wishing I was everywhere *except* for in my present season. These truths have enabled me to have and do it all in each season, primarily because they have helped keep me focused on today.

Fix Your Eyes on Jesus

Throughout every season of my Christian life, I have been able to stay focused and make the most out of each one because I made the decision long ago to fix my eyes on Jesus, His Word and His will for my life *daily*. I have learned that if my goal each day is to be more like Jesus as a wife, a mom, a leader, a speaker, a friend, a daughter and a sister, then so much of my having and doing it all falls into place.

Even through the difficult seasons, keeping my eyes fixed on Jesus helped me to see how God was using those tough times to mold and shape me into becoming more Christlike. This enabled me to embrace the season (sometimes a little unwillingly!) rather than resist it, despise it or try to skip over it. Admittedly, I haven't been perfect at this. There have definitely been times when I temporarily chose to focus on the pain, the frustration or the challenge of the season instead of on Jesus. As a result, instead of moving ahead in my having and doing it all, I moved toward the pain and frustration! Trust me, it's so much better (and quicker) to keep your eyes on Jesus regardless of the season.

Guard Your Heart

One of my life Scriptures is Proverbs 4:23, *"Keep and guard your heart with all vigilance and above all that you guard, for out of it flow the springs of life."*[2] Protecting our heart is so important that the Bible tells us to guard it above *all* that we guard! In the Hebrew, this word "guard" alludes to a very aggressive protest. So, it's not like the kind of guarding you might do when someone is trying to take a bite of your hamburger; it's the kind of bulldog tenacity by which you guard the last few bites of your piece of dark chocolate cheesecake!

It's no wonder God gives us such strong advice because *all* of our "all" flows out of our heart. When our heart is healthy, whole and right with God, then it won't be difficult to keep our destinies on course. But if we let our guard down and allow things like bitterness, unforgiveness, lust, greed, fear and anxiety to take root, our heart will become clogged, thus slowing or potentially halting our ability to flow smoothly from one season to the next. It's time to take an inventory of what kinds of things you might be harboring in your heart. Are there issues you have not dealt with? Have you allowed apathy to take hold? Lethargy? Insecurity? Allow the Holy Spirit to help bring healing to every part of your heart.

Anchor Your Soul

I remember being on a boat on the Mediterranean Sea when a sudden and rather brisk storm arose. The boat was rocking like crazy, yet the captain of the ship was as calm as could be. He had dropped the anchor, and as long as that anchor kept a firm hold, he knew his vessel would be fine. His confidence in the anchor brought me great comfort, as even though I've endured much airplane turbulence, I've not had too much experience with water turbulence. This little boat voyage was the perfect visual to the Scripture in Hebrews 6:19: *"This hope is a strong and trustworthy anchor for our souls. It leads us through the curtain into God's inner sanctuary."*[3]

As we pursue having and doing it all, there will most certainly be times when the circumstances around us get rocky. If our hope is in things, our position or what others think of us, we're likely to find that the "boat" of our life starts taking on water. Before we know it, we'll find ourselves shipwrecked. But if our hope is anchored in Jesus, we will never be moved.

Draw Near To God

I remember back when I was in Bible college, single, and able to spend three hours in prayer and study with God almost every day of the week. And then I got into full-time ministry... and then I got married...and then I had kids...and then...and then...and then... Believe me, I completely understand the dilemma of getting 1000 things accomplished each day and still carving out the time to spend with God. What Christian woman does not deal with this? But the fact of the matter is, if we are running so much that we have no time left to talk to God, we are way out of balance. Drawing near to our source of *everything* needs to be the highest priority if we want to have and do it all in life, and out of the 1000 things that need to be done, spending time with God must be at the top of our list.

Now before many of you start feeling all that guilt and condemnation, let me say this: throw out your legalism, find what works for you in *this* season of life, and stop feeling guilty about it! There is no correct formula for drawing near to God; you must simply do whatever you need to do to be close to Him.

James promises, *"Draw near to God, and He will draw near to you."[4]* When we take the time to nestle into our Father in heaven, we will find the strength, power, wisdom and contentment to navigate through every season of life.

Live By Design, Not Default

Have you ever stopped to think: Why am I doing everything I am doing? Is it God's plan for my life, or is it just what I think I'm supposed to do? Is my family involved in something simply because I'm afraid of what others will think of us if we're not? Is there anything I do *only* because it's what my mom did?

The frustration we often feel during certain seasons is due to the fact that we've never stopped to ask ourselves these kinds of questions. As a result, many women go through the seasons of their lives living by default instead of by God's design. If we live by default, then we will mechanically go through our lives feeling unsatisfied and uninspired. This is not God's plan (revisit Chapter 3 for inspiration). In terms of staying focused on each season, if we're simply doing what everyone else is doing, rarely (if ever) stopping to consider what it is God is asking us to do, we will inevitably be tempted to rush through certain seasons, or worse still, try to bypass them altogether.

When we enter every season of life understanding that it has been carefully designed by God as a vital step on our journey and part of our "all," we can then live each season with purpose and passion.

Rest

It's funny how fast life can get away from you, isn't it? A few years ago, I realized I had somehow managed to let my life get away from me. Nick and I were running like crazy to keep up with the growth of the ministry. We knew that if we didn't take time to stop and really replenish our bodies and souls, it was not going to be good for our marriage, kids or ministry. We learned the importance of making sure there were times and even seasons of rest and rejuvenation in between the seasons of busyness. It's the only way we will have the ability to have and do it all!

Sometimes we find navigating a particular season difficult simply because we're just plain tired! Here's some advice: Take a nap. Go and get a pedicure. Make all the kids have "quiet time," lock yourself in your bedroom and read a great book. Get out from your cubicle and fluorescent lights and go and take a walk outside on your lunch break. Meet a friend for coffee. Be spontaneous and leave the dishes until tomorrow morning and go have sex with your husband (sorry, single girls)! Do something today to find some personal refreshment, whatever that might be for you. Make sure that as you're taking care of everything and everybody else, you're also taking care of yourself!

Renegotiate Regularly

Don't you wish there was a perfect formula for having and doing it all? A chart that would tell us how to do each season, how long to stay in it, and when to move on to the next?

It would be so easy to stay focused if we knew exactly how long each season would last *and* if there was an accompanying handbook! There's no magic formula, but I can give you a key to ensure you won't get stuck in a season: renegotiate your life on a regular basis.

People, circumstances and seasons are continually shifting and changing, and to have and do God's "all," we must learn to change with them. What we did yesterday to succeed in a particular season will not necessarily work for us today or tomorrow. For instance, it would be unwise of me to think I could run as hard now as I did when I was in my early 20s. Having a husband and family to consider, my priorities have had to be refocused; certain things have had to be removed, whilst other things have been added. As my children grow, new doors open and we move into new seasons, we will have to adjust accordingly.

Having and doing it all is a constant process of change—a continual ebb and flow from one season to the next. To have and do it all, we must understand and transition through the seasons of life, remaining malleable, flexible and open to what God wants to do in and through us in every season.

it's all about relationships

chapter seven
it's all about relationships

"Christine, stop psychoanalyzing it!" After about three hours of mental gymnastics, I had finally come to the point where I was talking out loud to myself. Not a good sign. But still I went on, "It's no big deal...it's not a commitment, it's not a proposal, it's *coffee*! Does coffee even count as a date anyway? And it's not like it's with a movie or rock star; it's just with a normal guy named 'Nick.' Girl, you have to simmer down."

After checking myself out in the mirror for the zillionth time, I decided the best thing to do was to cancel. I mean, what was I going to tell all my girlfriends? For the last several years, I was the self-proclaimed founding president of the Single Until Rapture Club (SURC)...how could I possibly explain to the other members that I was going out on a date? We had formed the "group" (spearheaded by me, of course) not as some kind of feminist, anti-male, anti-marriage group, but simply because we were all in our late 20s, going full throttle in ministry, and had come to the conclusion that it was probably highly unlikely that any of us would ever slow down long enough to get married. So now, how could I, as their fearless leader, admit I was slipping in the ranks and going out for coffee with a guy from our church? Granted, he was a very good-looking guy, and one seemingly worthy of the slippage, but still...there was my pride after all (or was it fear?).

Before I knew it, I found myself riding in Nick's car on the way to coffee. I had every intention of canceling as soon as he showed up, but somehow in a flash of gentleman-like chivalry—not to mention amazing cologne—I couldn't find the words to turn him away. Instead, off we went, driving to a nearby coffee shop. Or so I thought. After about 20 minutes, I began to wonder where in the world this guy was taking me. Maybe I should have done some kind of police background check on him before I got into the car with him!

Just then, he pulled into a parking spot right outside my favorite café in Sydney. (How did he know?) This was a long way from where I lived and it was then I realized that he not only wanted to take me somewhere I loved, but also to a place that was unlikely to be filled with my friends, who would have found it difficult to resist spreading rumors or distributing the wedding invitations before the date was even over! *Clever guy,* I thought. *It won't be too bad spending a bit of time with him.*

And then "a bit of time" slipped into "hours" as we talked and talked and talked. We bantered back and forth about a broad range of topics. It was such a breath of fresh air to talk about something more than what my favorite band was, what was happening on the latest TV show, or how great the coffee tasted. Cute, clever *and* smart...my curiosity was piqued, and I found myself thinking I might like to spend some more time with this man. He must have read my mind because just then he said, "I happened to pack a picnic lunch if you are interested. There is a nice park across the way, and we could grab a bite." Cute, clever, smart *and* cunning...hmmmmm.

Nick was so nonchalant about his picnic lunch up-sell that there was no way for me to have been ready for the feast he'd prepared! He carried everything: the blanket, the basket and the entire cooler. And when he started taking all of it out, he looked like Mary Poppins magically pulling things out of her bag. He had five different kinds of breads, four selections of gourmet French cheeses, a delicious antipasto, a few types of meats and at least three different beverages! I wondered how this Bible college student could have afforded such an incredible spread, and how a man could even differentiate between five different styles of bread was beyond me! I was suitably impressed. I could definitely see myself spending more time with this guy.

For the next four hours, we sat together and talked. It was a perfect day...beautiful weather, great food, and stimulating conversation. I could feel my SURC crown begin to slip...

it takes all types

That first date with Nick reminds me of how crucial the right relationships are in order to truly have and do it all. I have dedicated an entire chapter to this subject, as too often we can underestimate the power and value of relationships in our lives (romantic or not). We must understand that our relationships will either help or hinder us from having and doing it all.

God created us with an intrinsic need for, and dependence on, relationships. No one was designed to do life alone. From the outset God said, *"It is not good for man to be alone, so I will make a suitable companion to help him."*[1] This is a reminder that not one of us can have and do it all without others. It is through godly, positive, life-giving relationships that we are encouraged, inspired, uplifted and carried. Importantly, these relationships can even challenge us to continue to pursue the purposes of God for our lives.

The first thing we must remember is to have life-giving relationships and not life-depleting ones. Some of us are struggling in life because we have allowed relationships to flourish that are full of toxic emotions such as negativity, criticism, comparison, jealousy, insecurity and fear. We can't pursue having and doing it all if we are constantly being weighed down and depleted by negative relationships.

We must proactively build those relationships that are a friend to our purpose and destiny. I encourage you to critically evaluate the relationships in your life and determine which ones have the biggest influence on you. Make sure they are helping and not hindering you. If you find that these relationships are not producing the fruits of the Spirit: love, joy, peace, patience, kindness, goodness, faithfulness, gentleness and self-control, then you need to reevaluate what place they have in your life.

the best kind of friends

One of the major reasons why I have been able to have and do it all is because of the great friends I have in my life. I intentionally and continuously surround myself with a great network of friends who support, love, inspire, encourage, and when necessary, challenge me. These friends are all different from each other in personality, interests and vocation, but singularly passionate in their desire for God's best. I spend a lot of time and energy investing into these specific friendships because I realize what a significant part they play in helping me to accomplish my destiny (and vice versa).

I can't help but smile when I think of how dynamic and unique each one of my friends is. Some of these girlfriends really step in and help me with my children, and oftentimes I wonder what I would do without them. Others are there when I need to process certain issues, let off some steam, or get a different perspective. Others still will challenge me to step it up and press in, while others love to shop and catch a movie with me. There are some friends with whom I could honestly just sit for hours and do nothing but laugh. *(By the way girls, if we are really going to have and do it all we so have to learn to laugh on the journey.)* There are so many wonderful rewards that come from fostering strong, healthy friendships—who would possibly want to have and do it all if the adventure didn't include great friends?!

It saddens me when I hear women say they can't be bothered building friendships because they feel that women are just too much drama and hard work. Look, I realize we girls definitely have the ability to be drama queens at times; however, we need to decide we're going to be the kind of women that are not high maintenance friends, but rather good, godly girlfriends. We need to resist the drama, comparison, backbiting, gossip and other negative traits and become each other's cheerleader.

single and loving it

As soon as we Greek girls leave the birth canal, we're being groomed for marriage. So for my mom, having to wait 30 years before she saw her daughter in a wedding gown and veil was excruciating...not to mention the pain I had to endure for all those years when well-meaning family would remind me that my biological clock was ticking—*fast*!

I had a lot of years to adjust to the fact that I was single, and as I said earlier, I truly believed that single was how I would enter eternity. So I know what it's like to walk into a room filled with gorgeous, happy couples only to have an old friend (and I use the term "friend" loosely) yell across the room, "So, Christine, have you found yourself a man yet?" *Oh Jesus, please let the ground open and swallow me up right now!* I would think. In addition, I don't know how many blind dates people would try to set me up on...and their only criteria would be that the man was breathing. Seriously, how desperate did these friends of mine think I was?

Regardless of the subtle (or not so subtle) pressure we may feel to hurry up and find "the man," it's one we should never succumb to outside of the plan of God. Numerous times I have come across women who hold back from pursuing their "all," waiting for their partner to come along and complete them. These girls somehow feel that unless they're married, they can't have and do it all.

In my experience, I've found that the more passionately you're pursuing your "all" as a single woman, the more likely it is that you will meet the right man, in the right season, who will continue to support and encourage you to have and do it all after you're married.

Imagine if I had been sitting on the sidelines with a secret desire to have and do it all, but waited until Nick married me to start pursuing it? Then once the honeymoon was over, I would really start to begin my sprint towards my destiny. He would have thought he married a different woman! But because I was already in the thick trenches of my having and doing it all, Nick has only ever known me as a woman who wants God's "all" for her life. In fact, it was because I was going after God with my "all" as a single woman he was attracted to me in the first place (besides, of course, my good looks!); so it was no surprise to him when I continued to do so as an engaged woman, and then as a married woman and now as a mother.

I *love* single and confident chicks. I have a team full of young unmarried women who are energetic, gifted, talented, healthy and passionate about Jesus and life—and they have an earnest desire to be married one day. Some are in their 30s and 40s, but they're not sitting around miserable and forlorn, waiting for their knight in shining armor to come and rescue them from their misery. In fact, they understand that their knight in shining armor actually came 2000 years ago in the form of Jesus. Because of that, they can have and do their "all" in this season *now*. These girls want to ensure that when they do meet "Mr. Right," they will have become who they need to be in order to embark on that season of their lives. They don't view singlehood as a barrier to having and doing it all. They have actually come to the realization that if you can trust God with your salvation, health, career, destiny, calling and finances, you can trust Him to bring you a life partner. Remember, our identity and purpose is found in Christ—not in another person. If you don't grasp this truth when you're single, you will always look to your spouse to complete you and make your "all" come to pass, but only God can do that.

Don't forget that Jesus was an example of how to be single and still fulfill God's "all" for your life. 1 Corinthians even advocates some benefits of being single: *"There is a difference between a wife and a virgin. The unmarried cares about the things of the Lord, that she may be whole both in body and in spirit. But she who is married cares about the things of the world – how she may please her husband."²* Of course, this Scripture is not saying it is better to be single than married, but it helps us to realize that life is not on hold whilst being single. Instead, it's a time where God can to do a deep work in us without other distractions. (Remember girls, we actually have to allow Him to do that work.)

it's all about relationships

the dating game

What girl doesn't remember her first real date? Every girl I've talked to has basically the same story. There's the planning of the perfect outfit followed by the flawless style of the hair, then the change to a different perfect outfit, and the ever-so-careful application of the make-up. Then it's off to the kitchen to eat a snack so as not to eat like a pig at dinner, meticulously ensuring nothing that might cause bad breath is consumed. Then there's the brushing and flossing of the teeth, changing into a completely new outfit which of course leads to a re-style of the hair and re-application of make-up. And to top everything off, there's the all-over mist of perfume followed by a final check in the full-length mirror...which may well lead to another clothing change, hair re-style, then make-up re-application! I have to say, I'm kind of looking forward to helping my girls get ready for their first dates...when they're 35 years old, of course.

When it comes to long-term relationships, the one that will most directly impact our capacity to have and do it all is the person we choose to marry. In my experience, many women panic because their partner hasn't come along during the timeframe they've allocated; so desperation sets in and they end up compromising or settling. Don't make this same mistake! Instead, use time to your advantage so you can choose wisely. Take it from a woman who waited until she was almost 30 to get married: if you're patient, and wait for the man God has designed just for you, you'll never, ever regret it.

So, how *do* you know whom you should date? Should you give the guy the time of day or send him along on his merry way? Girls all over the world ask me these kinds of questions and here's a little guide I give them. It's the "Is This the Guy for Me?" test:

- Does he love Jesus? (If he never told you he was a Christian, does he give you enough evidence to convict him of it?)

- Is he planted in a local church? (Again, not just warming a seat, but is he involved and serving in his local church?)

- What kind of relationships does he have with his family and friends? Are his closest friends Christian, and is he accountable to them? Does he honor and respect his parents?

- Does he have other godly men as mentors who can speak into his life?

- Is he a friend to your destiny, or will he take you from what you know God has called you to do?

- What kind of words does he speak? Is he a positive person, ready to encourage and build you up, or is he negative and quick to pick you apart?

- Is he afraid of hard work? Does he recognize that anything worthwhile takes work? And does he have a J.O.B.?

- Is he a man who is committed to personal growth and change? Does he address those areas of his life that may be weaknesses or does he ignore them?

- Is he more about building God's Kingdom or pursuing success for personal gain?

- Are you physically attracted to him? Not to get too carnal, but if there is no spark and the guy doesn't make you weak in the knees when he's around you, then he's probably somebody else's husband. If he feels more like a brother than a boyfriend, maybe he's not for you.

While going through this checklist, remember that nobody's perfect (after all, we're all on the journey of becoming like Christ), but determine that you will never settle for less than God's best for your life.

married and loving it

What happens when he has passed the test, pops the big question, and you say "Yes! Yes! Yes!"? Is that the pinnacle of having and doing it all? No—that's just the beginning, and in order to continue having and doing it all, you have to be committed to valuing and continually building the relationship.

The marriage relationship is definitely one that is under attack in our society, and therefore we must determine to work hard after the wedding day to ensure we continue to grow in love and pursue the purposes of God together.

The biggest thing we have to remember is that love is not the tickly feeling you get on the inside every time your new boyfriend holds your hand. I hate to break all the Hollywood stereotypes, but no, you will *not* love marriage all of the time. In the middle of a cold night when you go to sit down on the toilet only to realize (as you are falling in) that your husband forgot to put the seat down...love isn't quite the first feeling that springs to mind. But if your definition of love is derived from God's description in 1 Corinthians then yes, you *can* love marriage all the time because it's completely your choice.

Here's what that Scripture says: *"Love suffers long and is kind; love does not envy; love does not parade itself, is not puffed up; does not behave rudely, does not seek its own, is not provoked, thinks no evil; does not rejoice in iniquity, but rejoices in the truth; bears all things, believes all things, hopes all things, endures all things. Love never fails."*[3]

Notice that none of the descriptive words used are warm, fuzzy feelings; rather they're all action words that we can accomplish with or without the tickly vibrations. One of the greatest revelations I came to understand about marriage is I can love Nick whether I *feel* like it or not! It's a good thing too, because if either of us were just relying on our feelings as the ultimate barometer for our marriage, we probably wouldn't have made it past the first year! Feelings come and go, but as it says above, *"love never fails."*

Strong, healthy marriages don't just happen, they take conscious effort. Nick and I have implemented several standards in our relationship that help us to guard our marriage as well as keep things fresh. Here's five of them that may help strengthen and safeguard your marriage:

There's No Escape Clause

Once you say, "I do," you must settle in your heart that divorce is never an option. This is a lifetime commitment. Even if there's the smallest place in your heart reserved as an escape clause where you would consider leaving if your marriage got difficult, then it's very unlikely your marriage will make it. Obviously, if you're in a situation where you're being abused or in danger, you must go and find help. But your husband forgetting to wipe down the shower or not throwing his underwear in the dirty laundry pile isn't a cause for divorce.

It's so easy when we're in the honeymoon stage of marriage. All of his jokes are hysterically funny and even those smacking noises he makes when he chews are so cute and charming...and then the time goes by...his sense of humor begins to grate on us, and let's not even bring up the issue of the eating noises. We think, *Did I make the biggest mistake of my life? How could I ever have thought I could have made a marriage work with someone so different than myself?* Sadly some marriages never survive this stage because there is an unwillingness to put in the hard work needed to iron out all the kinks. But what we need to realize is that God brings two people together, oftentimes very different from each other, to see things through different perspectives.

While there are ways Nick and I are similar—vision for our family and ministry, commitment and love for Jesus etc.—there are lots of ways in which we differ. Just one amusing example is that in those first years of marriage, Nick always thought I was fighting with him because he came from a quiet, reserved family and communicated accordingly, while I came from a big, fat, *loud* Greek family where volume was a necessity in order to be heard. He'd often ask, "Chris, why are you yelling at me about this?" To which I would respond, "What do you mean, 'yelling?' This is just the way I talk!" By openly communicating and each of us having an openness to understand the other's perspective, we've made hundreds of adjustments in order to keep our marriage healthy.

No matter what the differences are or what challenges come our way, if we want to have it all in our marriages, we must settle in our hearts that there's no escape clause.

Understand Nobody's Perfect

Jesus is the only human to have ever walked perfectly on this planet, and the sooner we resolve this fact for ourselves the better! Not only will this realization help us have grace for our husbands when they disappoint us, but also for ourselves when we're the ones that blow it. Marriage is an alarming litmus test of how selfish and how imperfect we can all be.

By the time Nick and I got married, I had already established a strong daily routine. When I came home in the evenings, I was used to fixing my dinner (all the while on the phone talking about work), and then eating my dinner in front of my computer (continuing to communicate about work), and then go to bed with both my phone and laptop (in case anything would come up about work). I'll never forget the day early on in our marriage when I decided to ask Nick, "Honey, is there anything I could be doing that would make our marriage stronger?" He laughed and said, "Maybe, when we're together in the evenings, there could be a time when you turn off the computer and we could actually talk face to face." I was so involved in my own routine, I wasn't even aware I was doing that. I remember thinking, *Oh yeah! There is another person in this relationship besides myself!*

I tell this story because so often we can be very quick to point out our spouse's imperfections and never admit (or even notice) our own. I'm not perfect, he's not perfect, nobody's perfect. This being true, there will inevitably be times when we disappoint or let each other down. Rather than nag or nitpick (which we girls can be great at), let's have grace for each other and learn to communicate kindly and honestly about those issues that bother us.

Affair-Proof Your Marriage

Nick and I have simply decided that our marriage *is* the affair! We are consistently working to keep things fresh and exciting between us, and we go out of our way to express how much we love each other. Sometimes it's a fun text or a note hidden somewhere, and other times it's a surprise gift or date. There's rarely a time when we call and the other doesn't answer because our marriage is one of the highest priorities in our lives. (Really, it's second only to our relationship with God.) We realize that no matter how long we have been married, neither of us is immune from having an affair, so we do everything possible to create strong safeguards and habits to prevent such a disaster, including:

- When one of us is traveling, we make sure to talk a few times a day.
- We have strong, intimate friendships that keep us accountable.

- We have *no* secrets...and I mean *none*!
- We have great sex. (Enough said. I'll spare you the charts and graphs.)

Just like it's too late to protect your house against termites when they've already infested your property, affair-proofing measures need to be in place before a marriage is already on the slide. Be honest with each other about the conditions or situations that may lead to an affair and commit to habits and behavior that will keep things fresh and alive.

Find Aspects of Your Spouse to Love

Like I said before, during the honeymoon phase, it's so easy to notice all the things about your hubby that you just adore. And then life happens, kids happen, stretch marks happen, and his man-boobs start to take form! Now, all of a sudden, we begin to notice only those things we don't like about him. Throughout an entire marriage, we must constantly search for the aspects of his character, his surprise thoughtful gift (even if he still got the date wrong), the ways he takes care of things, *whatever it is* that we love and appreciate. These are the traits and characteristics we need to meditate on, not all the ways he might rub us the wrong way.

Husbands need love, support and encouragement from us, not nagging or complaining. If we'll communicate with him from a position of what he is doing great instead of how he always seems to be missing the mark, our husband will rise up and soar above our expectations and become the man God has called him to be. Let's affirm...not burn.

Discover New Things to Do Together

Boredom is a marriage carcinogen! Endless repetition will cause the most exciting of activities to become tired and dull. If you and your spouse are having the exact same conversations, arguments, financial challenges, the same routine sex, the same friends and watching the same television shows, it's very likely you guys are going to get bored! One thing is certain: bored people always end up looking for a way of adventure, and sadly, the adventure may not include you!

Shake things up a bit! Get a babysitter for the kids and go on an overnight trip somewhere. Try picking up a new hobby together. Drive a different way to church, eat breakfast for dinner, switch sides of the bed, do *something* that will break you out of your boring routine and reignite a fresh spark in your marriage. Your marriage can be the example of the strong, fulfilling, exciting marriage everyone around you wants to have. It takes work, but the rewards are so worth it!

Having and doing it all in life is absolutely no fun without amazing, life-giving relationships. In fact, without them, none of us will actually be able to experience everything in life God has for us! They are like a compass that helps us navigate through life successfully. We need great relationships in every season of life: as teenagers, young women, single, dating, when we're married, when we become parents... Let's not settle for mediocre relationships, but let's go for loving, healthy, powerful friendships—of all kinds—that will enrich us and strengthen us as we go after having and doing it all.

it's all about endurance

chapter eight
it's all about endurance

It was Catherine's baby dedication, and for years I had been inviting my family and relatives to come to a service at my church. Many of them had actually shown up, and all at the same time! Granted, it was in my favor that baptizing a baby is a huge event for Greeks, and while there would be no sprinkling of water that afternoon, I guess they all figured this was the closest thing they were going to get. So everyone gathered for the celebration, and I was excited *and* totally prepared! Catie was decked out in her dedication dress, matching bonnet, hat and shoes, and Nick and I were beaming.

Everything was going according to plan, that is, until we stood up to take Catie up on stage. She decided she just couldn't hold the contents of her stomach for another second, and she proceeded to projectile vomit all over her outfit *and* all over me! *Nice.* For a moment, I wished this was an actual baptism because both of us could have be dunked into a nice warm tub of water. I wondered which would be better: looking like drowned rats up on stage, or having to deliver a 30 minute message (did I mention I was actually preaching that day?) all the while smelling the wonderful aroma of puke? I chuckled to myself as we walked up the stairs to the stage because these kinds of things happen to me all the time! Just when I think everything is meticulously planned, something unexpected is bound to happen.

Like the time I was flying to Lafayette from Houston, and after boarding the plane, they discovered the wheels were broken. After sitting in the hot cabin for quite a long time, they moved everyone to another airplane so we could take off. Finally, the crew on the new plane informed us all to prepare for take-off. As we finally settled into our seats and received the clearance for take off, the control tower right behind us caught on fire! And when I say "caught on fire," I don't mean a little chimney smoke, I mean a full-on movie-like explosion with a million dollar special effects budget. Within what seemed like .5 nano-seconds, the entire runway was surrounded by fire trucks and men geared up to save the day. Okay, so maybe that's a slight exaggeration, but seriously, it was almost as if I had somehow been transported to the set of the crazy comedy *Trains, Planes and Automobiles*, where everything that could go wrong did go wrong! *So much for all that pre-travel intercessory prayer,* I thought as I ushered my two children out of the plane, *again*!

Or, how about the time I was in the middle of speaking at a women's conference and a baby started to cry. No big deal, right? I mean, I've been speaking for many years; this kind of distraction happens all the time. Except in *this* instance, I had recently had another baby, was smack bang in the middle of nursing season, and let's just say my schedule that particular day was such that I was overdue for a feeding. As a result, when my ears heard the sound of the baby's cry, the only thing my mammary glands perceived was: "Time to release the floodgates!" And so they did...right in the middle of my sermon.

During my time on this planet, I have come to realize one of the only certainties in life is there will always be uncertainty! And while I can laugh as I remember the stories above, I have to admit there have been many times in my life when uncertainty and unexpected circumstances have come and the results didn't necessarily become an anecdote to be laughed at later. Rather, they presented themselves as challenging trials and difficult times that had to be endured. These were circumstances that I hadn't planned for at all and ultimately had no control over. It was during these times that I had to make a conscious choice to allow the difficulty of the circumstance to strengthen my capacity to endure, rather than to weaken me and break my spirit.

The truth is, no matter how much we may try to plan out our lives and destinies to run along a perfectly straight path, life happens! And at some point, uncertainty confronts us all. Sometimes the uncertainty we deal with is mildly irritating and other times it seems to be almost physically painful and overwhelming. While the degrees may vary, like I said earlier, uncertainty is a constant. There is no use wasting our time wondering *if* we will face trials, because we all *will*. This is why the ability to endure is so critical to having and doing it all in life. The enemy does not want us to have and do it all, and he will ensure that we face circumstances designed to take us out of the race. Our capacity to endure determines whether we will overcome challenges and hardship or succumb to their pressure. When we choose to proactively develop and maintain the spiritual muscle of endurance, we will be able to continue to fulfill our God-given destiny and purpose... Even in the midst of inevitable obstacles and hurdles.

certain uncertainty

I'm more aware than ever before of the uncertainty and volatile nature that defines the world we live in today. It only takes a few minutes of flipping through a newspaper or watching a news broadcast to figure this out. We see terrorist attacks and political unrest in many nations around the world, global financial crises, environmental breakdown and social upheaval in many countries. In addition to the tumultuous situations facing the planet, each of us has our own private storms we have to navigate through from time to time.

As a student, mother, wife, boss, employee or the multiplicity of roles we play, we're inevitably going to face trials and periods of life when we simply don't know how in the world everything is going to work out. *How am I going to pay for college? My daughter just came home and told me she was pregnant... what do I do? What if my son never gives his heart to the Lord? What if my suspicions are correct, and my husband actually is having an affair? My doctor just diagnosed me with cancer. My business is close to bankruptcy and we don't know how to handle it. My kids are all teenagers...and learning to drive!*

I wish I could tell you that if you simply pray the right anointed incantation, then *poof* everything around you would magically fall into place; but the truth you already know is: there's no such prayer. Every single one of us is going to be confronted with uncertain times, stresses, tests and trials; it's actually a part of having and doing it all. Jesus told us in the book of John, *"In the world, you will have tribulation, but be of good cheer for I have overcome the world."[1]* Notice Jesus didn't say you *might* face problems, or you *probably won't but just in case...* He said you *will* be challenged by the storms of life.

This Scripture actually helps me realize that just because I'm going through a trial doesn't mean I've failed in some way, missed God's direction for my life or that I should shrink back from having and doing it all. As long as we're breathing, we're going to encounter challenges at one point or another along the journey of life. Endurance is an essential quality in facing and overcoming these challenges successfully. It's critical we learn how to endure rather than just merely survive these difficult times.

The book of James gives us a tremendous key about how to do this. He writes, *"My brethren, count it all joy when you fall into various trials, knowing that the testing of your faith produces patience. But let patience have its perfect work, that you may be perfect and complete, lacking nothing."[2]* I recognize this is probably not a Scripture that many of us have highlighted in our Bibles, or used as inspiration for a cross-stitched pillow. In fact, when many of us "faith" people hear this, what we actually hear is: "Count it all joy, blah, blah, blah, that you may be perfect and complete, lacking nothing." There are many important words between "joy" and "lacking nothing;" words which actually hold the keys to successfully dealing with the inevitable challenges life serves up.

Even in times of adversity, I've learned to count it all joy because I have come to understand that if I keep the right perspective and respond in the right way, then God can do a deep work *in* me so that He can do something *through* me.

When trials, tribulations, and seasons of uncertainty arise, our attitude is *everything*! If we look at the problem and only see difficulty, impossibility and hardship, we'll likely throw our hands up in defeat. Conversely, if we see these trials as an opportunity for God to do a great work *in* us as part of the process of having and doing it all, then this will fuel us to keep going, and fill us with the strength and passion to endure and overcome.

No matter what kind of circumstance you are facing right now, you have the ability to endure and come out on the other side stronger and better than you are today! I have found that during uncertain times, there are certain questions I choose to ask myself that help keep me focused, on track, and able to endure. I believe they can do the same for you.

Ask Yourself: What Am I Thinking About?

We women have the ability to fix our minds on 20 different things at a time; it's a God-given mechanism for juggling the zillion daily tasks at hand. It's actually quite an art when you think about it. We can be talking on the phone, solving the problems of the world, expertly changing a poopy diaper with only one wipe, performing the Heimlich maneuver on our other child who just swallowed a Lego and still notice the internal alarm sounding in our brain to take the tuna casserole out of the oven before it's scorched. On the flipside of this superpower, multi-tasking mindset is the fact that we can worry about 87 different things in about 13 seconds flat! *My son just failed his alphabet quiz in kindergarten, he'll probably be the kid everyone makes fun of, and how is he ever going to make it through college? I must not be parenting him well enough. I'm a failure as a mom! Or, I just saw a cute guy at Starbucks, and I wasn't wearing any make-up…what if the day I meet my husband I make the same mistake, or what if I have spinach in my teeth, or what if that day I have a terrible panty line? There is just no hope; I'm never going to get married! And on and on it goes…*

Proverbs tells us that as a *woman* (feminine emphasis mine) thinks in her heart, so is she.[3] In other words, our thinking actually determines who we are and what we become! Thus, in order to have and do it all, it is imperative we have the right mindset. Ultimately, our thoughts govern our actions, and our actions play a role in creating or shaping the environment we live in. If we are constantly thinking about how we'll never find a husband, how our kids will never obey us, how we never have enough money or how we'll never lose those extra pounds, we'll begin to act as though it's true, and before long these negative thoughts will become our reality.

The good news is that we can decide what our mindset is going to be! Colossians 3:2 commands us, *"Set your minds on things above, not on things of this earth.*"[4] How reassuring. We don't have to meditate on whatever thoughts and images happen to drop into our heads each day; we can make our thought life whatever we want it to be by choosing to "set our minds" on the right things. If it wasn't possible to do so, then God wouldn't have put it in His Word.

Essentially, there are two perspectives through which we can view every situation in life. One is the "heavenly" perspective that Paul exhorts us to set our minds on, and the other is the "worldly" perspective that he also warns us about. We have the power to transition our thinking out of the worldly per-spective and into a heavenly one. This isn't always easy at first. It takes practice and commitment to change your default mindset. This is why it is so critical that we're spending time in God's Word daily, and meditating on the *truth* it contains, rather than the facts of our current circumstances. We need to immerse our minds in His Word so we can quickly recall these principles during difficult moments or challenging seasons.

Romans 12:2 says, *"And do not be conformed to this world, but be transformed by the renewing of your mind, that you may prove what is that good and acceptable and perfect will of God."*[5] We all want to prove what is good and acceptable and the perfect will of God. After all, isn't that what having and doing it all is really all about—fulfilling our destiny?

But in order to *do* God's perfect will, we have to *know* what God's will is. This comes from a deep understanding of the Bible and personal revelation from the Holy Spirit. When we are fueled by God's Word, our thoughts inevitably become governed by His truth, and this truth causes us to be internally transformed. This transformation is what Paul is referring to when he exhorts us to renew our minds. It has an incredible effect on our actions and responses to people and circumstances. We begin to analyze situations from a heavenly perspective and react accordingly. It's amazing what the appropriate response can do for a seemingly hopeless situation. This is why truth has the power to *change* the facts.

Learning how to renew my mind has profoundly changed my life and helped me to move forward, even when seemingly devastating circumstances have presented themselves. In Chapter 4, I touched on a pivotal time in my life when I found out that I was adopted. The internal aftermath of that initial blow had left me so confused and hurt I didn't really know what to feel. When I did have time to actually process the information I had just been given, thoughts of worthlessness and rejection began to slowly make their way through my head. Immediately, with what seemed almost like a pre-programmed response, my spirit launched a counter attack against the enemy's attempt to take me out of my race. I found myself saying out loud: *"For you created me in my inmost being, you knit me together in my mothers womb. I praise you because I am fearfully and wonderfully made. Your works are wonderful, I know it full well."*[6] While the facts surrounding my adoption told me that someone didn't want me, the truth of God's Word reinforced that God had always loved and wanted me. Instead of spiraling down a path to self-destruction, God's Word enabled me to see my adoption from His perspective rather than my own.

Ask Yourself: Who Am I Listening To?

I was recently sitting in an airport (surprising, I know), surrounded by a large crowd of people. I had taken a moment to put my book down, and in just a matter of a few minutes I heard people giving dozens of opinions on different topics. But the odd thing was that the opinions the people were talking about weren't even their own! One lady was talking about Oprah's newest fad diet, another was giving Suzie Orman's latest philosophy on the stock market, another was giving Tim Gunn's fashion advice to her mother, and yet another was talking about what Bradgelina thought about the environment. I wondered how many of these people had any opinions of their own?!

In our fast-paced world driven by media and technology, we have the opportunity to access literally hundreds, thousands, and perhaps tens of thousands, of views on every imaginable issue. The real question is: are we actually taking the time to listen to what God thinks about these issues? It's fine to hear what the media or social commentators have to say about world events, but are we also seeking out what God thinks? On a more personal level, it's *okay* to listen to what our friends or our parents have to say about the situations happening in our lives, but more importantly, what's God saying to us about it? I think sometimes we get lost in the storms of adversity because we haven't stopped to listen to what God is speaking to our hearts, or to follow His directions about how to navigate through them.

Regardless of whether we are in a storm or not, it is so critical that biblical truth is the overwhelming sound in our lives. This is why every day, I do something to connect myself with Word of God. I'll read a Scripture, listen to a teaching CD, listen to a podcast, or simply meditate on a promise in His Word. I do this because I want God's truth to echo so loudly in my life that it drowns out the sound of any other contrary voice that could possibly distract or deter me.

In a world filled with conflicting messages about love, sex, career, purpose and beauty, we must always remember that God's perspective is our life-line. His truth is constant and unwavering, and it is only by knowing the truth of the Word of God that we can walk in the freedom to have and do it all. *"Then Jesus said to those Jews who believed Him, 'If you abide in My word, you are My disciples indeed. And you shall know the truth, and the truth shall make you free.'"*[7]

It's critical that we're listening to people who have a mature relationship with Christ and a firm foundation in His Word. We must ensure that the dominant voices speaking into our lives, whether it be our friends, mentors, teaching resources, or even what we're reading, align with the Word of God, otherwise we'll get off track. The voices that speak into our lives are essential to having and doing it all because they either enable us to sift through all the noise of this world and dispense with those messages contrary to biblical truth, *or* they will send us down a spiral path of confusion and discontentment.

Ask Yourself: What Am I Talking About?

We girls sure do know how to talk. We like to tell the story of our day, how we felt about everything that took place, what we think so-and-so thought about what we said to her, how we feel about what we think so-and-so thinks about us, what we think we will probably say to so-and-so the next time we see her so that we can make sure she truly understands what we were trying to say when we said that thing that we said... and then we take a much needed breath before we dive right back into more talking. We seem to have an innate word quota (which by the way, is usually much, much higher than our husband's quota) and if we don't fill that quota, then we feel somehow unfulfilled!

With all these words flying out of our mouths, do we ever stop to think what exactly it is we're saying? Are our words bringing life to our world, or are they bringing death? Proverbs says, *"Death and life are in the power of the tongue, and those who love it will eat its fruit."*[8] We frame our world with the words we speak. Words contain great power, and when an unexpected storm rises up to confront us, how well we endure it is often determined by the words we speak.

A few years ago, I was in the USA during their annual hurricane season, and one day I was watching the news as a very strong storm was about to make landfall. This particular reporter was standing outside in full rain gear, practically being blown over as the winds grew stronger and stronger. I began to wonder just how much this guy was getting paid to report this disaster. The winds were so intense that he was gripping on to a nearby pole for dear life. *Now that guy is committed!* I thought, *If only every Christian would be as dedicated to God's Word during crisis as this man is to reporting the news.*

This is a perfect picture of the posture we must have when the storms of life rise against us. The book of Hebrews says, *"Let us hold fast the confession of our hope without wavering, for He who promised is faithful."*[9] Just as this reporter held on for dear life to stop himself from being blown away, each one of us must hold fast to our confession of faith as our anchor when bad weather hurtles toward our life. This is not the time to pick up the phone and call Auntie Merriwether so you can whine and complain about your husband or lack thereof, or bemoan the impossibility of your financial struggles, or talk about how serious your health issues are and how you will probably die. I understand that sometimes the fear, doubt and uncertainty can feel overwhelming, but this is certainly not the time to use your word quota to reinforce those negative thoughts.

Remember the end of the above Scripture, *"...for He who promised is faithful."* God is faithful. Let's be careful to watch over our words and to choose wisely that which we allow to come out of our mouth. Instead of giving power to our fears, let's speak life over our situation, our finances, our family, our marriage, and our relationships. Our words are a creative force and through words of faith, we can speak life into every circumstance.

Ask Yourself: Where Am I Going?

Women know how to run, and I'm not talking about jogging. If we happen to catch sight of grey roots peeking out on our heads, we run to the salon for a cut and color. If we hear about a "one day only clearance" at the mall, we're out of bed at the crack of dawn, standing outside the store with our kids still crusty-eyed from the whirlwind wake-up call. And God forbid the household runs out of toilet paper, or even worse, chocolate! Quick as a flash, we run to the store to pick up a "few things." When we're in need of something, we girls know just where to go, and how to get it.

Just as we know where to go to meet our physical needs, we must also know where to go to meet our spiritual ones.

I'm certain that a significant reason I'm still on the journey of having and doing it all is because I have decided to stay planted in a local church and to be an active part of a dynamic, vibrant, life-giving community. It is here that I have found love, grace, encouragement, friendships, inspiration, healing, joy, family, protection and guidance. In some of my darkest hours, when I felt that I could endure no longer, it was the strength of my local church family that helped support me. If we're to have and do it all, then we must cultivate the habit of running to God and His house, and not from it, during times of adversity, challenge and disappointment.

If you're struggling with loneliness, or your boyfriend has just broken up with you, you don't need to run to a nightclub to find companionship, you need to run to the house of God. If your business is in the red, or your stocks just fell through the floor, don't run to Vegas to try and make back your nest egg, run to the house of God. If you've just found out your teenager is struggling with pornography, drugs or has to repeat the 9th grade, don't try to get your answers from a popular talk-show host who has never been a mom or a psychologist who has three failed marriages, run to the house of God and find strength from God-focused people raising great families. These are just a few examples of the many frustrations and difficulties we can face in life. While the specifics may differ for each of us, the constant is that God's house and His people are a source of strength, healing, community and direction.

I know some of these examples are fun and light hearted, (and often the cause of much angst in our lives) but if you are confronting much more serious issues, the best way to effectively process and work through them may be ongoing counseling and support. If this is the case, then I urge you to enlist the help of a great, strong, reputable Christian counselor for God's perspective and wisdom. There is no shame in seeking out help, direction and perspective when it comes to overcoming hurdles in our lives.

Ask Yourself: What Am I Remembering?

I'm not going to lie to you; sometimes I can have a very selective memory. Like when Nick and I are having a "passionate discussion" about a particular topic, and I realize he's wrong, I can remember exactly what he said, how he said it, what he was wearing, where he was standing and what we ate for lunch later that day. But when the tables are turned, and I realize *I'm* the one who is mistaken, my memory can tend to get a bit murky. "Huh? What? Ummm...yeah...I can't seem to recall anything about that day. Nick, are you sure you didn't dream up that conversation?"

So often, we can have the tendency to vividly remember those things we ought to forget and completely forget those things we ought to remember! But in running the race of having and doing it all, choosing to remember the right things can help us to have great endurance...especially during the difficult seasons of life.

Let's make the choice to remember the good and not the bad. We can choose to remember and dwell on the incredible things God has already done in our lives, rather than get so wrapped up in the problems of today, along with the junk that happened yesterday, and the negative stuff that we think *might* happen tomorrow!

Whenever I'm tempted to give up having and doing it all rather than choosing to endure and persevere, I usually pull out old journals and prophetic words that I've received over the years to remind myself of God's faithfulness and specific promises to me. This helps me to recall all of the good things God has done, and how He has never left or forsaken me. So if He hasn't done it before, why would He do it now? I also focus on all the things He has blessed me with including a wonderful husband, two beautiful daughters, an incredible spiritual family, a fantastic team, great friends, a home, a ministry and internal healing and restoration.

Every time I look back on the timeline of my own story, I see God's grace, redemption and protection in my life. It's so important we remember where we have come from, but even more importantly, that we remember the personal defining moments where God has exhibited His faithfulness. These will help to carry us through difficult seasons and give us the strength to endure the future challenges we may face.

Ultimately, we must never forget that trials and struggles *will* come our way. It doesn't mean that we've blown it, or that our spiritual lives are a wreck. Uncertainty is a constant in life, but it doesn't have to prevent us from having and doing it all. When you choose to endure rather than throw in the towel when times get tough, there's one thing for certain—you are on your way to fulfilling your God-given destiny.

it's all about longevity

chapter nine
it's all about longevity

I couldn't believe my eyes as I sat watching the documentary on the television. The lengths to which these people were going to conquer a physical epidemic that has plagued the earth since the beginning of mankind was incredible! Maybe my inability to peel my eyes away from the show was because it was 3am and my body was in one of its near-incoherent jet-lag stupors, or maybe it was simply a case of morbid curiosity. Or perhaps my fascination could be attributed to the fact I had just turned 40, and I had my own thoughts about how I too would one day face the inevitable condition described in this show. Either way, I don't think I had ever seen this many surgical procedures before as these patients were going to extremes to overcome a disease that would only continue to spread to every individual on earth: a disease called aging.

I was confused. *Aging is now considered a disease? Isn't it just a normal progression of life on this earth?* As the documentary explained all the symptoms of this "disease," and the plethora of natural and medical remedies to fight it, I think I aged 10 years just stressing out about which one of these options I should choose! They talked about dozens of anti-aging prescriptions and treatments, along with the medicines available to deal with the side effects of these remedies. Listed among them were different Botox treatments, creams, liposuction and facelifts...not to mention the brand new surgical procedures for all the *other* body parts I never even knew could be surgically lifted, reduced or augmented. *Really? There are people out there who actually feel they need buttock implants?! I wonder if they take donors...*

I was amazed at what the people featured in the documentary chose to do in pursuit of eternal youth. One of these was a woman who started off looking beautiful, but in the end looked oddly doll-like with her shiny, saran wrap skin, strangely large eyes, tiny nose, overly pouty lips and very, very, *very* white teeth. Now don't get me wrong: I'm certainly not against anti-aging products or even cosmetic surgery (I'm pretty sure I've tried at least half of the skin creams out there!), but I wondered why this woman felt the need to go to such extreme lengths with her money, time and body in order to fight something that was inevitably going to happen anyway. At one point in the interview, she even admitted that although she looked younger than her own daughter, she still didn't feel any younger on the inside than she did prior to all of her alterations.

All of a sudden, I realized my face had been scrunched the whole time I was watching the program, which made me even more self-conscious of the fact that the wrinkles on my face must be deepening by the minute. I grabbed a compact mirror out of my purse to check if my furrowed brow and squinting eyes had done any permanent damage. I couldn't tell. *Should I run out right now and try to find the latest and greatest OTC super-duper-antioxidant-biotanical-animopeptide-grapeseed serum with a UV Protection of 7500? I bet I could find a 24-hour drugstore around the corner...*

I was just about to throw on my running shoes (I thought I could multi-task and reduce facial signs of aging *and* burn some calories at the same time!) when Nick woke up and asked me what in the world I was watching. I think I over-whelmed him with a waterfall of information about this new-found "disease," how we both needed to start planning for our cosmetic futures, the many options available to us, and whether he wanted to get his shoes so he could take a run with me to the drugstore.

All I can say is thank God for great husbands because he im-mediately turned off the television and asked me where the real Christine happened to be. I started laughing because just hearing the sound of his voice snapped me back into sanity and out of the endless mental vortex of whirling thoughts about how I could look 25 years old and not a day over! Through a new set of eyes (not from any surgery but from a different mindset), I began to tell Nick all about the program: how be-cause of our obsession with this unattainable goal of turning back the hands of time, the world has created a $45 billion anti-aging industry to meet our growing demands, needs and desires, and how even though many of the people's external appearance changed because of the various procedures, there was rarely, if ever, a corresponding internal change.

The quest for eternal youth has become somewhat of an addiction in today's society. We all want to hold onto the energy, agility and sense of adventure we felt in our younger years. Who can blame us? Sadly, so many of us have bought into the lie that we can achieve this by ensuring we remain young-looking rather than approaching youth from a biblical perspective. True youth is determined by our internal spirit, not by our outward appearance.

The Bible says, *"The Lord does not look at the things man looks at. Man looks at the outward appearance, but the Lord looks at the heart."*[1] The spiritual condition of our heart plays a significant role in our ability to actually have and do it all. Proverbs teaches us *"to guard our heart above all else, for it determines the course of our life."*[2] If our heart is vibrant, youthful, energetic and healthy, then we'll have the internal fortitude to fulfill our purpose and go the distance.

As we already know, the having and doing it all life is not a moment in time when we have arrived at a particular destination, but rather a lifelong journey of having all God has for us in order to do all God has purposed for us to do. Girls, this is going to take longevity, which is going to require stamina, which in turn is going to take a strong and youthful spirit within us.

In my life, I do a tremendous amount of travel. I have often had to walk straight off a plane and onto a platform to speak.

Needless to say, there have definitely been times I've learned the hard way how critical it is for me to keep my body fit and healthy. I'm very conscious about my diet, sleep patterns and water intake because I realize that it ultimately doesn't matter how young I am in spirit; it's little good if I don't have a physical body to carry that young spirit around in.

The importance of physical fitness is not an issue of vanity, but rather one of longevity. We need to make sure we take full advantage of all of the information about how to live healthy lives that is so readily available to all of us via books and the Internet. However, in doing so, let's be careful not to buy into the world's view of what a healthy body is supposed to look like.

Being healthy and maintaining a youthful spirit is not about having a particular pants size, bra size or some Hollywood movie star body type; it's just about finding what works best for each one of us, and sticking to a personal plan (just as we all have a unique purpose, we also have unique bodies). As Christian women, let's be healthy and strong role models for other young women to follow.

forever young

One of my personal heroes in the Bible is Caleb. Admittedly, the older I get, the more inspired I am by his fervor, tenacity, faithfulness and relentless pursuit of the purposes of God until his dying breath.

When the spies were sent in to Canaan, it was Caleb who came back with a spirit of faith and said, *"Let us go up at once and take possession, for we are well able to overcome it."*[3] He was 40 years old at this stage, and committed passionately to having and doing God's "all" for his life. He was surrounded with negativity and fear, but he never lost sight of his "all."

Even when Caleb was forced into the wilderness for 40 years because of the murmuring, grumbling and complaining of the children of Israel, his fire or enthusiasm wasn't quenched. After entering the Promised Land, Caleb could have settled, entered retirement and lived a quiet, safe, risk-free and peaceful life. In fact, many would have thought he deserved to just sit back and relax. But Caleb had a different spirit in him.[4] He kept pursuing God.

A fundamental key to having and doing it all is that we actually continue to pursue it all throughout the entirety of our life. It's precisely the spirit and heart attitude that Caleb demonstrated that we require in order to run our race and finish our course.

It's no surprise that when Caleb was 85 years old and could have cashed in his "pension fund," he said: *"So here I am today, eighty-five years old! I am still as strong today as the day Moses sent me out; I'm just as vigorous to go out to battle now as I was then. Now give me this hill country that the LORD promised me that day. You yourself heard then that the Anakites were there and their cities were large and fortified, but, the LORD helping me, I will drive them out just as he said."*[5]

spiritual age checkup

One of my favorite parts of that documentary on the anti-aging industry was the segment about the many symptoms of aging. They listed 45 certain signs of this condition, and I had to laugh because I remember thinking how I have at least half of them! It was hilarious to me because these "symptoms" were in fact just normal occurrences that happen to the physical body as it is subject to time, the natural elements, stress and most of all, gravity!

As I thought more about these symptoms, I realized that several of these signs could also indicate when our inner self is starting to spiritually sag. Whilst it's easy to stand in front of a mirror and see the obvious ways our skin and body are aging, it's much more difficult to recognize when our spirit is getting older, duller, and just plain worn-out. So just as we can go to the doctor to have a physical checkup, here is a list of symptoms that can serve as our own personal spiritual checkup.

Loss of Flexibility

I'm constantly amazed at the contortions our girls are able to accomplish with their little bodies. They are incredibly malleable as they sink into the splits and then strike poses with their legs behind their heads. And then they ask Mommy and Daddy if we want to try! While I consider myself to be in pretty good physical shape, I certainly am not as flexible as I used to be, and I would never dream of getting on the floor with them to attempt some of their body pretzel postures. Although my body may not be quite as flexible as it was when I was a child, I endeavor to keep my spirit extremely flexible through regular spiritual stretching.

Having and doing it all will take a flexible spirit. We have to keep stretching and expanding on the inside, otherwise God will never be able to use us to do bigger and better things. For those of us who have had babies, think labor! Just when you think you have nothing left to stretch, the Holy Spirit serves as our midwife and whispers, "Just a little longer, and just a bit more." In other words: *"Enlarge the place of your tent, and let them stretch out the curtains of your dwellings; do not spare; lengthen your cords, and strengthen your stakes. For you shall expand to the right and to the left, and your descendants will inherit the nations, and make the desolate cities inhabited."*[6]

If we allow ourselves to get too comfortable and stiff (picture me trying to get into my daughter's pretzel pose...on second thoughts, no, don't), never wanting to stretch into new levels of life, we will hinder so much of what God has planned for us. He has great exploits for us to accomplish, but it's up to us to keep growing, changing and enlarging if we want to see these plans come to pass.

Let's be like Caleb and *never* allow inflexibility to cause us to settle, atrophy or lose our youthful zeal.

Diminishing Vision

I'm not going to deny it; I love to tease all my friends who have come to the place in their lives where they need glasses to read everything. I ever-so-modestly rub in the fact my vision is still

20/20, and even today, I can read any book, no matter how small the typeface, *without* having to hold it at arm's length. Yes, there may come a day when all of this gloating will come back to haunt me, but for the moment, I'm enjoying having this light-hearted banter with them. The fact is that as our physical bodies age, one of the first signs is a diminished ability to see!

Similarly, a key indicator for growing old spiritually (as opposed to maturing) is that we start to lose sight of God's long-term vision for our lives. Proverbs tells us *"where there is no prophetic vision, the people cast off restraint."*[7] If we are to have and do it all, we can't afford to cast off restraint; in fact, we must learn to "wear" the constraints of our vision. The vision must be an on-going, unfolding, prophetic revelation so that we don't get distracted or settle for short-term gratification. Some of us desire to be married, have a family, live in a dream home or work in a dream job; but don't stop when these things become a reality, because in and of themselves, they're not the goal—having and doing God's all for our life is the goal. We must consciously choose to continue to look up and forward and pursue His purpose.

There are many other factors that are directly related to the condition of our heart, that can diminish, impair or otherwise affect our vision. For example, if we don't deal with the inevitable disappointment and discouragement that comes up on the journey, we'll begin to lose heart and lose sight of the greater vision. Unforgiveness, offenses, bitterness, jealousy, envy, greed and the like can cause calluses to form, which, if we could see into the spirit realm, are like scales or cataracts forming over our spiritual eyes. So let's choose to keep our spiritual sight clear by daily fixing our eyes upon Jesus, the author and finisher of our faith.

Hearing Loss

It's uncanny to me how I can be at a playground with my girls, send them off to play amongst dozens of children, and if one of my daughters calls for me, I'm able to decipher her call instantly among the throngs of screaming, excited children. When Catie or Sophia yell for me, I can hone in on their voices and respond immediately. We all have this ability with certain voices and people in our lives, don't we? As our bodies age, however, our ability to hear and interpret sounds can diminish, and everything can start to sound muddy and indecipherable.

In Luke 8:8, Jesus cried, *"He who has ears to hear, let him hear!"*[8] and we are exhorted throughout the Scripture to constantly have an ear inclined to the voice of the Spirit. In order to have and do it all, we need to be able to decipher the voice of God from all of the other voices that are vying for our attention Let's be real—never in history have we been bombarded by so many voices. There are 7.3 million new pages being added to the World Wide Web today, and even more will be added tomorrow. One thousand books will be published today, and the total of all printed knowledge will double in the next five years. If we were to start reading right now, and continue reading for 24 hours a day, 365 days a year, we would never catch up with everything being written. There are five billion instant messages that will be sent today. Our world will make available more information in the next decade than has been discovered in all of human history.[9] I could go on, but I think you get the picture.

So pardon the graphic illustration, but in order to have and do it all, we must ensure that we regularly remove the "wax" from our spiritual ears that can build up over time so that our ability to hear God's voice is not dulled. If we fail to monitor the other voices screaming for our attention, we can inadvertently miss the voice of God. Ultimately, this is the only voice that will lead us into our destiny.

Loss of Energy, Strength and Speed

As I travel through airports, it is inevitable that every time I have to make a tight connection, Murphy's Law kicks in. I always seem to get stuck behind a company of *slooooooooowwwww* people on their way to a group tour. This of course means they're blocking the *entire* terminal, causing a human maze for anyone wishing to pass by to navigate through, which isn't helped by the fact they are all wearing matching tour t-shirts! And then, once I ever-so-politely weave my way through the crowd, and begin to race down the moving walkways, I'm stopped in my tracks because there's another distracted group of women clogging the passageway as they are chatting excitedly about their upcoming cruise to Bora Bora. In my haste, I want to shout, "Can you not see the signs requesting the standers to move to the right so the sprinters can get through on the left?" But, reminding myself that I'm a Christian, I refrain and wait patiently for the motorized runway to end...so can i have and do it all, please?

I can zip past them before the next one starts!

I'm sure that if we could see the world from God's perspective, we would see many people spiritually ambling in slow motion through life or getting distracted and stopping altogether. Some of these people may have one time or another been speeding along in the fast lane, but along the way they decided to take the scenic route to eternity!

Often, when we begin our pursuit of having and doing it all, we're full of passion, energy, enthusiasm and we run full steam ahead. After some months or years, it is not unusual to hear comments like, "I'm feeling burnt out," or "I'm just so tired of dealing with my husband and kids," or even, "I just need to take some time to pull back from everything." We feel empty, frustrated, weary, depleted and on the verge of a meltdown, ready to give up. There are many reasons for this, but I believe it can be boiled down to the simple fact that we try to do in our own strength what only God can do. Let's take heart from Galatians 6:9 which reminds us to *"not grow weary while doing good, for in due season we shall reap if we do not lose heart."*[10]

There's nothing wrong with pacing ourselves—there's a big difference between simply taking time to find rest and refuel because we've been running so hard, and feeling weary in our soul because we've been doing things in our own strength.

The Message Bible sums this thought up perfectly, *"Let me put this question to you: How did your new life begin? Was it by working your heads off to please God? Or was it by responding to God's Message to you? Are you going to continue this craziness? For only crazy people would think they could complete by their own efforts what was begun by God. If you weren't smart enough or strong enough to begin it, how do you suppose you could perfect it?"[11]*

These are strong words from the Apostle Paul, but it helps to keep it all in perspective. Only God can complete what He started in us. Our strength and source of completion is not found in our "all," or in other people, nor things, position or title. It's only to be found in Christ. The Apostle Paul reminds us to *"...be confident of this very thing, that He who has begun a good work in you will complete it until the day of Jesus Christ."[12]* God has started this work in us, and only He is able to finish it.

Tastelessness

Finally, the documentary talked about the fact that as we get older, our ability to taste things changes or diminishes. Growing up in a Greek household, and eating some of the best food this world has to offer, I can't imagine a worse symptom of aging! Seriously, if there ever comes a day when I can't tell the differences between souvlaki and mousaka, or pastitsio and baklava...I think I will become very good at fasting! How boring if all food tasted exactly same. Who would even bother to eat at all?

In a spiritual sense, we need to ask ourselves if our "taste" for God and our destiny is as sweet, intense and full of flavor as it once was? Or does our daily life have the equivalent taste of a bland bowl of high fiber bran cereal?!

If you're feeling like parts (or all) of your life have faded into tastelessness, you can change it! We all have the ability to get our spiritual taste buds back and to be refilled with joy and excitement for life. Joy is a fruit of the Spirit and is something we can choose to allow the Holy Spirit to develop, or continue to develop, in us.

You see, there's a direct correlation between us relishing the God-journey we're on and the aftertaste we leave in our relationships with others. Let me put it this way: my mother always used to tell me how important salt was when cooking because she could make a dish go from bland to vibrantly tasty with just a pinch. Well, as Christians, we're supposed to be the "seasoning" in every situation, circumstance or relationship we find ourselves in. Matthew 5:13 says, *"Let me tell you why you are here. You're here to be salt-seasoning that brings out the God-flavors of this earth. If you lose your saltiness, how will people taste godliness? You've lost your usefulness and will end up in the garbage."*[13]

What taste is left in people's "mouths" after an encounter with you? Did they taste the goodness of God through your words and actions, or were they left with a bitter aftertaste?

I have said it several times already, but it's so important that it's worth repeating: this having and doing it all life is not just about you and your destiny, it's about the people we encounter along the way and being a beacon that shows them the way to Jesus.

In the end, it all comes back to our relationship with Jesus. Psalm 34:8 tells us to taste and see that the Lord is good.[14]

When you taste of God's goodness, then you can't help but add flavor to your world as well.

We can have and do it all. The fountain of youth really does exist... It's found in our total reliance on Jesus, His strength and power. Whilst our physical bodies may fade with time, our spirits can stay young, vibrant, passionate and enthusiastic. And when our race on earth is done, having pursued wholeheartedly having and doing it all, our spirits will continue to live on forever in eternity.

If we wait upon God, the author of our life, we can run our race and finish our course, and complete all that He has set before us:

> *"Have you not known? Have you not heard? The everlasting God, the Lord, the Creator of the ends of the earth, does not faint or grow weary; there is no searching of His understanding. He gives power to the faint and weary, and to him who has no might He increases strength [causing it to multiply and making it to abound]. Even youths shall faint and be weary, and [selected] young men shall feebly stumble and fall exhausted; But those who wait for the Lord [who expect, look for, and hope in Him] shall change and renew their strength and power; they shall lift their wings and mount up [close to God] as eagles [mount up to the sun]; they shall run and not be weary, they shall walk and not faint or become tired."[15]*

What a promise...

Selah.

epilogue

epilogue

Hey Girlfriend,

As I sit here on yet another airplane, coffee in hand, reading over this manuscript and wondering how to end this, I have to tell you...I am at a loss. Not at a loss for words ("speechless" and Christine are mutually exclusive terms!), but it's more that I don't really think there's a nice and neat way to wrap a book like this up for you...

Just a second...the stewardess is standing in front of me, wearing a yellow safety vest and an oxygen mask, and although I have heard the safety message a trillion times, her proximity to my seat compels me to feign attention!

...and it's a good thing I tuned in, as the airline stewardess' well-rehearsed take-off speech has provided me with the perfect thought to help "land" this book.

Whilst the majority of flights I have been on are uneventful, and the most difficult decision I have to make is whether I want a wholegrain roll or sourdough bread with my meal, there have been times I've been in the air flying through the worst turbulence imaginable. It's in those scary in-flight moments that I desperately recollect Suzie the stewardess' safety message...

1. Life vest under the seat [check]
2. Put on oxygen mask first before assisting others [check]
3. Know where the exits are [check]
4. Place yourself in the brace position [check]

Okay, you may be wondering why on earth I am rambling about aircraft safety in the epilogue to this book. Good question. Let me explain. Although you will have finished reading it in just a few moments from now, the having and doing it all life is not about arriving...it's always about taking off on another God-adventure! And like with any adventure, there are new things to negotiate, seasons to endure, twists and turns to navigate. There will be days (the vast majority) that life will be exciting, but others that are downright scary.

Some of what you have read in these pages may apply to your life right now, whilst other chapters are a word for your future, so think of this book as an airline safety card. Reread it, apply it...and when turbulence hits, you'll know instinctively how to brace yourself and get into position to weather whatever comes your way.

Know too that the chief pilot (God) has everything under control. Even in the midst of what may seem like the toughest storm, if we will simply trust God with our life, and listen for His instruction, we'll undoubtedly hear Him whisper in our heart: *"Yes, daughter, right now having and doing it all seems impossible. But just stick with Me because when you have Me in you—surrounding you, ahead of you, and behind you—nothing is impossible!"[1]*

Girls, this is our opportunity to write our chapter in history. To go places and do things that preceding generations of women could have only dreamed possible. We have a responsibility to our generation to pursue having and doing it all, and to blaze a trail for the generations of women to come after us. Every effort, every sleepless night, every stretch of faith (even the painful ones), every mountaintop and even every valley is so worth it!

So in the immortal words of Suzie the Stewardess:

"Ladies, we are about to take off to have and do it all in life. Remember to stay in your own seat, and you must strap yourself in because whilst the view at 35,000 feet is breathtaking, there will probably be some turbulence along the way. Make sure your seat back and tray tables are in their upright position, and that all your carry-on luggage is stowed away. (You never know when the Captain is going to tell you to sprint to a new door of opportunity and you certainly don't want anything obstructing your path.) Now sit back, order a beverage, and enjoy the ride..."

Love,

Christine
xxx

acknowledgements

As always, I want to thank my family who know that when I go into the "book zone," there are many sacrifices to be made. It is because of their sacrifice that you have this book in your hands.

Nick, you are the most amazing husband and best friend. Thank you for always believing in me...especially when I don't.

Catherine and Sophia, I hope and pray that my example inspires you to always pursue God's "all" for your lives.

Thank you to my senior pastors and friends, Brian and Bobbie Houston. You have always encouraged and inspired me to dream bigger dreams, never settle, and pursue having and doing God's "all" for my life. Thank you for taking the limits off!

Joyce Meyer, thank you for being a forerunner and inspiration to a whole generation of us younger women. You have always believed in me and in many ways have empowered me to have and do it all. Thank you for sharing your wisdom and life with me as a spiritual mother.

My dear friend Molly Venzke, who dared to jump into the book bubble with me, your ability to take the boring and mundane and make it hysterically funny is a gift from God. This book would not be what it is without you.

Annie and Natalie, can you believe we did it again...and survived...and are still friends...and are caffeine addicts...and are sleep deprived...and are still pursuing it all? I could not imagine doing life without you both.

Maria, even from the other side of the world, you were still (as always) an integral part of the finished product. Thank you for your genius.

James, you are so loyal and faithful. I think you know more than you ever wanted to know about how a woman can have and do it all. Words cannot express my gratitude to you.

Jenn, Sarah, Maree and Kristen, thank you for taking the time to go over the manuscript. Your thoughts, comments and suggestions were critical.

references

Chapter 1:
1. Matthew 6:33 (NASB)
2. Ephesians 2:10 (AMP)
3. John 16:7 (NKJV)

Chapter 2:
1. Loren Cunningham, David Joel Hamilton & Janice Rogers. *Why Not Women?: A Fresh Look at Scripture on Women in Missions.* (YWAM Publishing, 2000)
2. Ibid.
3. Genesis 1:27 (NIV)
4. Genesis 2:23 (NIV)
5. Genesis 2:18 (NKJV)
6. Luke 8:1-3 (NKJV)
7. Galatians 3:27-28 (AMP)

Chapter 3:
1. Ecclesiastes 3:11 (AMP) – emphasis mine
2. Psalm 139:13-16 (MSG)
3. 2 Corinthians 10:12 (NKJV)

Chapter 4:
1. John 1:12-13 (NKJV)
2. Ephesians 2:8-9 (NKJV)
3. Romans 6:11 (NKJV)
4. John 17:19 (NIV)

5. 2 Corinthians 5:17 (NIV)
6. 1 Peter 2:9 (NIV)
7. 2 Corinthians 5:19 (NIV)
8. John 8:36 (NKJV)
9. Galatians 2:16 (NIV)
10. Ephesians 1:4 (NIV)
11. Ephesians 1:5 (NKJV)
12. Ephesians 1:6 (NKJV)
13. Ephesians 4:32 (NKJV)
14. Ephesians 1:11 (NKJV)
15. Ephesians 2:6 (NKJV)
16. Ephesians 2:10 (NKJV)
17. 1 Peter 5:10 (NKJV)
18. Romans 8:37 (NKJV)
19. John 16:33 (NKJV)
20. Hebrews 13:5 (AMP)
21. Romans 3:22 (NIV)
22. John 10:10 (NKJV)

Chapter 5:
1. Matthew 22:37-40 (NKJV)
2. Matthew 11:28-30 (AMP)
3. Hebrews 12:1-2 (NLT)
4. Psalm 23:1-3 (NKJV)
5. Galatians 1:10 (NLT)
6. Galatians 6:4 (NIV) – emphasis mine
7. Philippians 4:6-7 (NKJV)

8. 1 Thessalonians 5:17 (NKJV)

9. Philippians 3:12-14 (NKJV)

Chapter 6:

1. Ecclesiastes 3:1 (NLT)

2. Proverbs 4:23 (AMP)

3. Hebrews 6:19 (NLT)

4. James 4:8 (NKJV)

Chapter 7:

1. Genesis 2:18 (GNT)

2. 1 Corinthians 7:34 (NKJV)

3. 1 Corinthians 13:4-8 (NKJV)

Chapter 8:

1. John 16:33 (AMP)

2. James 1:2-4 (NKJV)

3. Proverbs 23:7 (NKJV)

4. Colossians 3:2 (NKJV)

5. Romans 12:2 (NKJV)

6. Psalm 139:13-14 (NIV)

7. John 8:31-32 (NKJV)

8. Proverbs 18:21 (NKJV)

9. Hebrews 10:23 (NKJV)

Chapter 9:

1. 1 Samuel 16:7b (NIV)

2. Proverbs 4:23 (NLT)

3. Numbers 13:30b (AMP)

4. Numbers 14:24 (AMP)

5. Joshua 14:10-12 (NIV)

6. Isaiah 54:2-3 (NKJV)

7. Proverbs 29:18 (ESV)

8. Luke 8:8 (NKJV)

9. Dave Ferguson. *The Big Idea*. (Zondervan Publishing, 2007)

10. Galatians 6:9 (NKJV)

11. Galatians 2:2-3 (MSG)

12. Philippians 1:6 (NKJV)

13. Matthew 5:13 (MSG)

14. Psalm 34:8 (NKJV)

15. Isaiah 40:28-31 (AMP)

Epilogue:

1. Matthew 19:26 (NLT)

A sought after speaker around the world, Christine Caine is passionate about the God life and seeing the local Church flourish across the earth.

Christine is a gifted communicator with a heart for reaching the lost and helping people unlock their God-given potential.

She is known for her "tell-it-like-it-is," passionate, and often humorous way of communicating profound messages of hope and inspiration.

Together with her husband Nick, and daughters Catherine and Sophia, Christine spends much of the year travelling to reach the lost, strengthen leadership, champion the cause of justice and build the local Church globally.

Christine Caine in a nutshell:

passionate::enthusiastic::inspirational::determined:: relentless::devoted::compassionate::authentic::creative:: innovative::caffeinated::greek::australian::traveling-preacher-chick::wife::mother::speaker::activist::blogger::author:: mentor::fighter of human trafficking::die-hard for the cause of Jesus Christ! (For more details go to www.chriscaine.com)

Follow Chris around the world in real time·

:: FACEBOOK   :: TWITTER
:: BLOG   :: MYSPACE
:: PODCAST   :: PHOTO GALLERY
:: NEWSLETTERS   :: MP³ DOWNLOADS

Connect online and join the adventure!

www·chriscaine·com

Every ³⁰ seconds, another person becomes a victim of human trafficking...

Let's do something about it!

The A²¹ Campaign is fighting the injustice of human trafficking.

Anyone can join - everyone can make a difference.

www.theA²¹Campaign.org

Equip & Empower Ministries is a proud supporter of The A²¹ Campaign